The Message of 2 Timothy

Guard the Gospel

John R. W. Stott

Rector Emeritus of All Souls' Church, Langham Place, and
Director of the London Institute for Contemporary Christianity

Inter-Varsity Press
Leicester, England
Downers Grove, Illinois, U.S.A.

Inter-Varsity Press
38 De Montfort Street, Leicester LE1 7GP, England
P.O. Box 1400, Downers Grove, Illinois 60515, USA

Inter-Varsity Press, England, is the book-publishing division of the Universities and Colleges Christian Fellowship (formerly the Inter-Varsity Fellowship), a student movement linking Christian Unions in universities and colleges throughout the United Kingdom and the Republic of Ireland, and a member movement of the International Fellowship of Evangelical Students. For information about local and national activities write to UCCF, 38 De Montfort Street, Leicester LE1 7GP.

InterVarsity Press, USA, is the book-publishing division of InterVarsity Christian Fellowship, a student movement active on campus at hundreds of universities, colleges and schools of nursing in the United States of America, and a member movement of the International Fellowship of Evangelical Students. For information about local and regional activities, write Public Relations Dept., InterVarsity Christian Fellowship, 6400 Schroeder Rd., P.O. Box 7895, Madison, WI53707–7895.

Text set in Great Britain
Printed and bound in Great Britain by
Dotesios Ltd, Trowbridge, Wiltshire.

UK ISBN 0-85110-737-0 (paperback)
USA ISBN 0-87784-295-7 (paperback)
USA ISBN 0-87784-925-0 (set of The Bible Speaks Today, paperback)

22	21	20	19	18	17	16	15	14	13	12	11	10
11	10	09	08	07	06	05	04	03	02	01	00	

General preface

The Bible Speaks Today describes a series of both Old Testament and New Testament expositions, which are characterized by a threefold ideal: to expound the biblical text with accuracy, to relate it to contemporary life, and to be readable.

These books are, therefore, not 'commentaries', for the commentary seeks rather to elucidate the text than to apply it, and tends to be a work rather of reference than of literature. Nor, on the other hand, do they contain the kind of 'sermons' which attempt to be contemporary and readable, without taking Scripture seriously enough.

The contributors to this series are all united in their convictions that God still speaks through what he has spoken, and that nothing is more necessary for the life, health and growth of Christians than that they should hear what the Spirit is saying to them through his ancient—yet ever modern—Word.

J. A. MOTYER
J. R. W. STOTT
Series Editors

CONTENTS

ACKNOWLEDGMENT

The biblical text in this publication is from the Revised Standard Version New Testament, Second Edition copyright © 1971, by the Division of Christian Education, National Council of the Churches of Christ in the United States of America, and used by permission.

PREFACE

DURING the last five years I seem to have lived inside this second letter of Paul to Timothy. In imagination I have sat down beside Timothy and have tried myself to hear and heed this final charge from the ageing apostle. I have also tried to share its message with many people: with the congregation of All Souls' Church, Langham Place in the autumn of 1967; with about 9000 students at the great Urbana missionary conference in the United States in December 1967; with those attending the 1969 Keswick Convention; with groups of pastors at various times in America, Wales, Ireland, New Zealand, Australia and Singapore; and with some Anglican bishops before the 1968 Lambeth Conference. On each occasion I have been impressed afresh by the timeliness for today of what the apostle writes, especially for young Christian leaders. For our era too is one of theological and moral confusion, even of apostasy. And the apostle summons us, as he summoned Timothy, to be strong, brave and steadfast.

The words which crystallize the letter for me are the two little monosyllables *su de* ('but as for you'), which occur four times. Timothy is called to be different. He is not to yield to the pressures of public opinion or conform to the spirit of his age, but rather to stand firm in the truth and the righteousness of God. In my judgment nothing is more needed by Christians in today's world and church than this same courage.

I express my warm gratitude to my secretary, Frances White-head, for her efficient and tireless labours during the past seventeen years, not least in the typing of innumerable manuscripts. She is not likely to forget this one, since it was the indirect cause of an accident which involved her in the pain of a dislocated toe!

J. R. W. STOTT

CHIEF ABBREVIATIONS

AG   *A Greek–English Lexicon of the New Testament and Other Early Christian Literature* by William F. Arndt and F. Wilbur Gingrich (University of Chicago Press and Cambridge University Press, 1957).

Alford   *The Greek Testament*, a Critical and Exegetical Commentary, by Henry Alford. Vol. III (Rivington, Fourth edition, 1865).

AV   *The Authorized* (King James') *Version* of the Bible, 1611.

Barrett   *The Pastoral Epistles* by C. K. Barrett (*The New Clarendon Bible*, Oxford University Press, 1963).

Calvin   *The Epistles of Paul to Timothy and Titus* by John Calvin, 1548 (Oliver and Boyd, 1964).

Ellicott   *The Pastoral Epistles of St. Paul* by C. J. Ellicott, 1861 (Longmans, Fourth Edition, 1869).

Eusebius   *The Ecclesiastical History* by Eusebius, Bishop of Caesarea, 4th century AD. Translated by H. J. Lawlor and J. E. L. Oulton (S.P.C.K., 1927).

Fairbairn   *Commentary on the Pastoral Epistles* by Patrick Fairbairn, 1874 (Oliphants and Zondervan, 1956).

Guthrie   *The Pastoral Epistles* by Donald Guthrie (*Tyndale New Testament Commentaries*, Tyndale Press and Eerdmans, 1957).

Hanson   *The Pastoral Letters* by A. T. Hanson (*The Cambridge Bible Commentary on the New English Bible*, Cambridge University Press, 1966).

Hendriksen   *The Epistles to Timothy and Titus* by William Hendriksen (Baker Book House, 1957 and Banner of Truth Trust, 1959).

JB   *The Jerusalem Bible* (Darton, Longman and Todd, 1966).

JBP   *The New Testament in Modern English* by J. B. Phillips (Collins, 1958).

LS   *Greek–English Lexicon* compiled by H. G. Liddell and R. Scott. New Edition by H. S. Jones (Oxford University Press, 1925–40).

Lock   *The Pastoral Epistles*, a Critical and Exegetical Commentary, by Walter Lock (*The International Critical Commentary*, T. and T. Clark, 1924).

MM   *The Vocabulary of the Greek Testament* by J. H. Moulton and G. Milligan, 1930 (Hodder and Stoughton, 1949).

Moule   *The Second Epistle to Timothy* by Handley C. G. Moule (*The Devotional Commentary* series, Religious Tract Society, 1905).

NEB   *The New English Bible* (New Testament, 1961; Old Testament, 1970).

Plummer   *The Pastoral Epistles* by Alfred Plummer (*The Expositor's Bible*, Hodder and Stoughton, 1888).

RSV   *The Revised Standard Version* of the Bible (New Testament, 1946; Old Testament, 1952; revised edition, 1971).

Simpson   *The Pastoral Epistles* by E. K. Simpson (Tyndale Press, 1954).

White   *The Pastoral Epistles* by Newport J. D. White (*The Expositor's Greek Testament*, Hodder and Stoughton, 1910).

INTRODUCTION

BISHOP Handley Moule confessed that he found it difficult to read Paul's second letter to Timothy 'without finding something like a mist gathering in the eyes'.[1] Understandably so. It is a very moving human document.

We are to imagine the apostle, 'Paul the aged', languishing in some dark, dank dungeon in Rome, from which there is to be no escape but death. His own apostolic labours are over. 'I have finished the race,' he can say. But now he must make provision for the faith after he has gone, and especially for its transmission (uncontaminated, unalloyed) to future generations. So he sends Timothy this most solemn charge. He is to preserve what he has received, at whatever cost, and to hand it on to faithful men who in their turn will be able to teach others also (2:2).

In order to grasp the letter's message and feel its full impact, it is necessary to understand the background against which it was written. Four points need to be made.

1. This is a genuine letter of Paul to Timothy.

The genuineness of the three Pastoral Epistles was almost universally accepted in the early church. Allusions to them occur possibly in the Corinthian letter of Clement of Rome as early as c. AD 95, probably in the letters of Ignatius and Polycarp during the first decades of the second century, and certainly in the works of Irenaeus towards the end of the century. The Muratorian Canon, which dates from about AD 200, ascribes all three letters to the apostle Paul. The only exception to this testimony is the heretic Marcion who was excommunicated in AD 144 in Rome. But he had theological reasons for rejecting these (and other)

[1] Moule, p. 16.

New Testament letters, and Tertullian expressed surprise that he had omitted the Pastorals from his canon. Eusebius in the fourth century included them among 'the fourteen epistles of Paul' which 'are manifest and clear (as regards their genuineness)', the fourteenth being the Epistle to the Hebrews which (he added) some rejected as not Pauline.[1]

This external witness to the authenticity of the Pastoral Epistles continued as an unbroken tradition until in 1807 F. Schleiermacher repudiated 1 Timothy, and in 1835 F. C. Baur rejected 2 Timothy and Titus as well. Since then scholars have ranged themselves on each side of the debate, and the Pastorals have had both powerful critics and doughty champions. For an elaborate critique the reader is referred to P. N. Harrison's *The Problem of the Pastorals* (1921), and for a careful defence of the traditional Pauline authorship to the commentaries by William Hendriksen (pp. 4–33) and Donald Guthrie (pp. 12–52 and 212–228). The issues can only be sketched here.

The right place to begin is to recognize that in the first verse of each of the three letters the writer advances a clear and solemn claim to be the apostle Paul. He goes on to refer to his former persecuting zeal (1 Tim. 1:12–17), to his conversion and commission as an apostle (1 Tim. 1:11; 2:7; 2 Tim. 1:11) and to his sufferings for Christ (*e.g.* 2 Tim. 1:12; 2:9, 10; 3:10, 11). More than that, the personality of the apostle seems to permeate these letters. Handley Moule wrote of 2 Timothy: '*The human heart* is in it everywhere. And fabricators, certainly of that age, did not well understand the human heart.'[2] Hence even those who deny the Pauline authorship of these letters tend to believe that the writer has incorporated genuine Pauline fragments in his work.

The first ground on which the Pauline authorship of the Pastorals is questioned is *historical*. It is argued that since they mention visits by Paul to Ephesus and Macedonia (1 Tim. 1:3), Crete and Nicopolis (Tit. 1:5; 3:12), Troas, Miletus and Rome (2 Tim. 1:17; 4:13, 20) which cannot be reconciled with Luke's record in Acts of the apostle's journeys, therefore these must be the author's fabrication or at best genuine visits which he has ingeniously misplaced. But if the apostle was released from his

[1] Eusebius, III.3.5.   [2] Moule, p. 21.

Roman imprisonment and then resumed his travels (as he expected and tradition says), before being re-arrested, it is perfectly possible to reconstruct the order of events (as we shall soon see) without any need to accuse the author of fiction or romance.

The second argument is *literary*. Critics reject the Pauline authorship of the Pastorals on the ground that much of their vocabulary is absent from the other ten letters attributed to Paul (and some from the whole New Testament), while many characteristic Pauline expressions in those ten letters are absent from the Pastorals. There are plenty of 'Paulinisms' in the Pastorals, however, both of style and of language, and the changes of time, situation and subject-matter are sufficient to account for the peculiarities. 'Great souls are not their own mimes,' as E. K. Simpson justly comments.[1]

The third and *theological* argument takes various forms. Some claim that the God of the earlier Pauline letters (Father, Son and Holy Spirit) and the grace-faith-salvation-works syndrome have become subtly changed and no longer ring true. But there can be no doubt that the Pastorals set forth the electing, redeeming initiative of 'God our Saviour' who has given his Son to die as our ransom and to rise again, and who now justifies us by his grace and regenerates us by his Spirit, in order that we may live a new life of good works. Others urge that the prevalent heresy which lies behind the Pastorals—its denial of the resurrection, its love of asceticism, its 'myths' and its 'genealogies'—is the developed Gnosticism of the second century, perhaps of Marcion himself. This conjecture ignores, however, the *Jewish* aspects of the heresy (*e.g.* Tit. 1:10, 14; 3:9; 1 Tim. 1:3–11) and its evident similarities to the Colossian heresy to which the apostle has already addressed himself a year or two previously.

The fourth argument is *ecclesiastical*, namely that the church structures envisaged in the Pastorals are those of the second century, including the monarchical episcopate to which Bishop Ignatius of Antioch referred in his letters. Some critics go further and find the whole atmosphere of the Pastorals too 'churchy' for Paul. Ernst Käsemann[2] quotes Martin Dibelius as having once said that the Pastoral Epistles 'mark the beginning of the bourge-

[1] Simpson, p. 15.
[2] *Jesus Means Freedom* (SCM, 1969), p. 88.

ois outlook in the church'. He adds that he cannot himself regard as Pauline letters in which the church has become 'the central theme of theology', 'the gospel is domesticated' and Paul's image is 'heavily daubed by church piety'.[1] One can only reply that this is an extremely subjective judgment. Paul's earliest letters already give evidence of a high doctrine of the church and the ministry, and Luke tells us that it was his policy to ordain elders in every church from his first missionary journey onwards (Acts 14:23). That he should have developed this further in the Pastorals, with instructions about the selection and appointment of ministers, the worship of the church and the maintenance of doctrine, is entirely understandable. But the church and ministry he describes are still recognizably the same, and there is no monarchical episcopate or threefold ministry yet, because 'bishops' and 'elders' are still the same order.

Consequently, the conclusion of many scholars is still that the arguments which have been advanced to deny the Pauline authorship of the Pastoral Epistles—historical, literary, theological and ecclesiastical—are not sufficient to overthrow the evidence, both external and internal, which authenticates them as genuine letters addressed by the apostle Paul to Timothy and Titus.

2. *The Paul who wrote it was a prisoner in Rome.*

He describes himself as 'our Lord's prisoner' (1:8), and this was his second Roman imprisonment. He was not now enjoying the comparative freedom and comfort of his own hired house, in which Luke takes leave of him at the end of the Acts and from which he seems to have been set free, as he expected. Instead, he was incarcerated in some 'dismal underground dungeon with a hole in the ceiling for light and air'.[2] Perhaps it was the Mamertine prison, as tradition says. But wherever he was, Onesiphorus succeeded in finding him only after a painstaking search (1:17). He was certainly in chains (1:16), 'wearing fetters like a criminal' (2:9). He was also suffering acutely from the loneliness, the boredom and the cold of prison life (4:9–13). The preliminary hearing of his case had already taken place (4:16, 17). Now he

[1] *Jesus Means Freedom* (SCM, 1969), pp. 89, 97.
[2] Hendriksen, p. 234.

was awaiting the full trial, but was not expecting to be acquitted. Death appeared to him inevitable (4:6–8). How had this come about?

It seems that, after being released from his earlier imprisonment (the house arrest in Rome described at the end of Acts), Paul 'again journeyed on the ministry of preaching'.[1] He went to Crete where he left Titus behind (Tit. 1:5), and then to Ephesus where he left Timothy behind (1 Tim. 1:3, 4). He may well have gone on to Colosse to see Philemon, as he had planned (Phm. 22), and he certainly reached Macedonia (1 Tim. 1:3). Of the Macedonian cities he visited, one will have been Philippi (Phil. 2:24). From Macedonia he addressed his first letter to Timothy in Ephesus and his letter to Titus in Crete. He told Titus his intention to spend the winter at Nicopolis (Tit. 3:12), a town in Epirus on the west (Adriatic) coast of Greece. Presumably he did this, and presumably, as he requested, Titus joined him there. If the apostle was ever able to fulfil his great ambition to evangelize Spain (Rom. 15:24, 28), it must have been in the following spring that he set sail. Clement of Rome in his famous letter to the Corinthians (chapter 5) said that Paul had 'come to the extreme limit of the west'. He may have been referring only to Italy, but an allusion to Gaul or Spain—and even Britain (as some have suggested)—seems more likely.

It is safe to assume that he later kept his promise to revisit Timothy in Ephesus (1 Tim. 3:14, 15). From there his itinerary seems to have taken him to the nearby port of Miletus, where he had to leave Trophimus behind ill (2 Tim. 4:20), to Troas (the port from which he had first set sail for Europe) where he stayed with Carpus and left his cloak and some books behind (2 Tim. 4:13), to Corinth where Erastus left the party (2 Tim. 4:20; cf. Rom. 16:23), and so to Rome. Somewhere on this journey he must have been re-arrested. Was it at Troas, explaining why he had no opportunity to collect his personal belongings together but had to leave them behind in Carpus' house? Or was it only when he reached Rome? We do not know the circumstances. But we do know that he was again arrested and again imprisoned, that this time he had to endure great hardship, and that there was to be no escape. For the Neronian persecution was in full swing

[1] Eusebius, II.22.2.

(AD 64). And the tradition is likely to be correct that Paul was condemned to death and then beheaded (as a Roman citizen would have been) on the Ostian Way about three miles outside the city. Eusebius quotes Dionysius of Corinth that Paul and Peter 'were martyred both on the same occasion', though he adds that Paul's execution was by beheading and Peter's (at his own request) by crucifixion 'head-downwards'.[1]

Shortly before he died, during his further and more severe imprisonment, Paul sent this second message to Timothy. His execution seemed to him imminent, so that he was writing under its shadow. Although it was an intensely personal communication to his young friend Timothy, it was also—and consciously—his last will and testament to the church.

3. *The Timothy, to whom the letter was addressed, was being thrust into a position of responsible Christian leadership far beyond his natural capacity.*

For over 15 years, since he had first been recruited in his home town Lystra, Timothy had been Paul's faithful missionary companion. He had travelled with him throughout most of the second and third missionary journeys and had been sent during them as a trusted apostolic delegate on several special missions, *e.g.* to Thessalonica and Corinth (1 Thes. 3:1 ff.; 1 Cor. 4:17). He had then accompanied Paul to Jerusalem (Acts 20:1–5) and may have been with him on the perilous voyage to Rome. At all events, he was certainly in Rome during the first imprisonment, for the apostle bracketed Timothy's name with his own when he wrote the prison Epistles to Philemon, the Philippians and the Colossians (Phm. 1; Phil. 1:1; 2:19–24; Col. 1:1).

It is not just that Paul had a strong affection for Timothy as a friend whom he had evidently led to Christ, so that he could call him his 'beloved and faithful child in the Lord' (1 Cor. 4:17). It is also that he had grown to trust Timothy as his 'fellow-worker' (Rom. 16:21) and his 'brother and God's servant in the gospel of Christ' (1 Thes. 3:2). Indeed, because of Timothy's genuine concern for the welfare of the churches and because of the loyalty with which 'as a son with a father' he had served with Paul in

[1] Eusebius, II.25.5,8 and III.1.2.

the gospel, Paul could go so far as to say 'I have no one like him' (Phil. 2:20–22). Among all Paul's associates Timothy was unique.

It is not surprising, therefore, that when the first imprisonment was over Paul left Timothy in Ephesus as the accepted leader of the church, a kind of embryonic 'bishop'. Wide responsibilities were given him: to combat the heretics who were troubling the church there, to order the church's worship, to select and ordain its elders, to regularize the relief and ministry of its widows, to command and teach the apostolic faith, together with the moral duties which flow from it.[1] And now still heavier burdens were about to fall on Timothy's shoulders. For Paul was on the point of martyrdom, and then the task of preserving the apostle's teaching intact would be his in yet greater measure. Yet, humanly speaking, Timothy was hopelessly unfit to assume these weighty responsibilities of leadership in the church.

For one thing, Timothy was still comparatively young. Paul had urged him in his first letter: 'let no one despise your *youth*' (1 Tim. 4:12). And in his second letter a year or two later he warned him to 'shun *youthful* passions' (2 Tim. 2:22). We do not know his precise age. If he had been about 20 years old when Paul enrolled him as a missionary associate, he would be in his mid-thirties now. This period of life was regarded as belonging to youth, 'for there were only two recognized standards of age to the Greek or Roman, *neos* and *gerōn*, *juvenis* and *senex*, and the former of these conveyed no such juvenile implication as our term *youngster* . . . It was employed of adults in the full vigour of life and of soldiers of military age to the verge of forty.'[2] Certainly the thirties would be a young age for such church leadership as had been committed to Timothy.

Next, Timothy was prone to illness. In his first letter to him the apostle referred to his 'frequent ailments', though without specifying what they were. He went on to recommend a tonic. For his stomach's sake, he advised, he should give up drinking only water and try a little wine as well (1 Tim. 5:23).

Thirdly, Timothy was timid by temperament. He seems to

[1] See the contents of Paul's First Letter to Timothy, with its varied instructions to a church leader.
[2] Simpson, p. 8.

have been naturally shy. If he had lived in our generation, I think we would have described him as an 'introvert'. He evidently shrank from difficult tasks, so that Paul in writing to the Corinthians had to pave the way for his mission: 'When Timothy comes, see that you put him at ease among you.' Again, 'let no one despise him' (1 Cor. 16:10, 11). Several times in this second letter which the apostle wrote him, he exhorted him to take his share of suffering and not to be afraid or ashamed, since God had not given us a spirit of cowardice (*e.g.* 2 Tim. 1:7, 8; 2:1, 3; 3:12; 4:5). These admonitions were evidently necessary. Paul knew Timothy's weaknesses. He could not forget his tears when they had parted (2 Tim. 1:4). In Fairbairn's words, Timothy was 'disposed to lean rather than to lead'.[1]

This, then, was Timothy—young in years, frail in physique, retiring in disposition—who nevertheless was called to exacting responsibilities in the church of God. Greatness was being thrust upon him, and like Moses and Jeremiah and a host of others before and after him, Timothy was exceedingly reluctant to accept it. Is someone who is reading these pages in a similar situation? You are young and weak and shy, and yet God is calling you to leadership? This letter has a special message for all timid Timothys.

4. Paul's preoccupation in writing to Timothy was with the gospel, the deposit of truth which had been revealed and committed to him by God.

The apostle's own career of gospel-work was virtually over. For 30 years or so he had faithfully preached the good news, planted churches, defended the truth and consolidated the work. Truly, he had 'fought the good fight, . . . finished the race, . . . kept the faith' (2 Tim. 4:7). Now nothing awaited him but the victor's wreath at the winning post. A prisoner now, he would be a martyr soon.

But what would happen to the gospel when he was dead and gone? The emperor Nero, bent on suppressing all secret societies, and misunderstanding the nature of the Christian church, seemed determined to destroy it. Heretics appeared to be on the increase. There had recently been an almost total Asian apostasy

[1] Fairbairn, p. 314.

from Paul's teaching (2 Tim.1:15). Bishop Moule goes so far as to write that 'Christianity . . . trembled, *humanly speaking*, on the verge of annihilation'.[1] Who, then, would do battle for the truth when Paul had laid down his life? This was the question which dominated and vexed his mind as he lay in chains, and to which in this letter he addressed himself. Already in his first letter he had pleaded with Timothy to keep safe the deposit: 'O Timothy, guard what has been entrusted to you' (1 Tim. 6:20). But since then the situation had worsened. So the apostle's appeal became more urgent. He reminded Timothy that the precious gospel was now committed to *him*, and that it was now *his* turn to assume responsibility for it, to preach and teach it, to defend it against attack and against falsification, and to ensure its accurate transmission to the generations yet to come. In each chapter Paul returned to the same basic concern, or some aspect of it. Indeed, we may summarize the message of the letter in terms of a fourfold charge:

Chapter 1: The charge to guard the gospel.

Guard the truth that has been entrusted to you by the Holy Spirit who dwells within us (1:14).

Chapter 2: The charge to suffer for the gospel.

Take your share of suffering as a good soldier of Jesus Christ . . . Remember Jesus Christ . . . as preached in my gospel, the gospel for which I am suffering and wearing fetters like a criminal (2:3, 8, 9).

Chapter 3: The charge to continue in the gospel.

Evil men and impostors will go on from bad to worse, deceivers and deceived. But as for you, continue in what you have learned and have firmly believed . . . (3:13, 14).

Chapter 4: The charge to proclaim the gospel.

I charge you in the presence of God and of Christ Jesus . . .: preach the word, be urgent in season and out of season, convince, rebuke, and exhort, be unfailing in patience and in teaching (4:1, 2).

[1] Moule, p. 18.

The church of our day urgently needs to heed the message of this second letter of Paul to Timothy. For all around us we see Christians and churches relaxing their grasp of the gospel, fumbling it, in danger of letting it drop from their hands altogether. A new generation of young Timothys is needed, who will guard the sacred deposit of the gospel, who are determined to proclaim it and are prepared to suffer for it, and who will pass it on pure and uncorrupted to the generation which in due course will rise up to follow them.

Chapter 1

THE CHARGE TO GUARD THE GOSPEL

BEFORE the apostle reaches the principal theme of this chapter, the charge to Timothy not to be ashamed of the gospel but rather to guard it safely (verses 8–14), he begins his letter with the customary personal greeting (1, 2), followed by a thanksgiving (3–5) and an exhortation (6–8). In this opening paragraph we are introduced in a very vivid way to both Paul and Timothy, the writer and the recipient of the letter. In particular, we are told something of how each man had come to be what he was. These verses throw light on the providence of God, on how God fashions men into what he wants them to be.

1. PAUL, AN APOSTLE OF CHRIST JESUS (verse 1)

Paul, an apostle of Christ Jesus by the will of God according to the promise of the life which is in Christ Jesus.

In styling himself 'an apostle of Christ Jesus' Paul is advancing a considerable claim for himself. He is in fact ranking himself with the Twelve whom Jesus personally selected out of the wider company of his disciples. To them he gave the special title 'apostles' (Lk. 6:13), indicating that he intended to send them out on their mission to represent him and to teach in his name. In order to equip them for this role, he arranged for them to be 'with him' (Mk. 3:14). They would thus have unrivalled opportunities to hear his words and see his works, and so be in a position to bear witness to him and to everything they had seen and heard of him (Jn. 15:27). He also promised them an extraordinary inspiration of the Holy Spirit to remind them of what he had taught them and to lead them into all the truth which he had not been able to teach them (Jn. 14:25, 26; 16:12, 13).

To this select group Paul claims that he was later added. He saw the risen Lord on the Damascus road, which gave him the qualification every apostle needed, to be a witness to the resurrection (Acts 1:21-26; 1 Cor. 9:1; 15:8, 9). Indeed, his Damascus road experience was more than his conversion; it was his commissioning as an apostle. Christ said to him: 'I have appeared to you for this purpose, to appoint you to serve and bear witness to the things in which you have seen me and to those in which I will appear to you, delivering you from the people and from the Gentiles—to whom I send you to open their eyes . . .' (Acts 26:16-18). For the Lord's words 'I send you' were *egō apostellō se* 'I apostle you', that is, 'I appoint you the apostle to the Gentiles' (*cf.* Rom. 11:13; Gal. 1:15, 16; 2:9).

This commissioning Paul could never forget. He defended his apostolic mission and message against all his detractors, insisting that his apostleship came from Christ and not from men (*e.g.* Gal. 1:1, 11, 12). Even now, at the moment of writing, humiliated by men and awaiting the emperor's pleasure, this common prisoner is a privileged apostle of Christ Jesus, the King of kings.

Paul goes on to describe his apostleship in two ways, reminding Timothy of both its origin and its object.

Its origin was 'the will of God'. He has used identical words (*dia thelēmatos theou*) at the beginning of both his letters to Corinth and of the two prison letters to the Ephesians and Colossians. Indeed, in nine out of thirteen of his letters, including his first (to the Galatians) and his last (this one to Timothy), he refers either to the 'will' or the 'call' or the 'command' of God by which he had been made an apostle. It was his sustained conviction, from the beginning to the end of his apostolic career, that his appointment as an apostle had come neither from the church, nor from any man or group of men. Nor was he self-appointed. On the contrary, his apostleship originated in the eternal will and historical call of almighty God through Jesus Christ.

The object of his apostleship concerns 'the promise of the life which is in Christ Jesus'. That is to say, he had been commissioned as an apostle first to formulate and then to communicate the gospel. And the gospel is good news for dying sinners that God has promised them life in Jesus Christ. It seems particularly appropriate that, as death stares the apostle in the face, he should here define it as a 'promise of life'. For this is what it is. The gospel offers men life—true life, eternal life—both here and hereafter. It declares that this life is 'in Christ Jesus', who not only said he was himself the life (Jn. 14:6) but, as Paul will soon elaborate, actually 'abolished death and brought life and immortality to light through the gospel' (10).

The gospel does more than 'offer' life; it 'promises' life to all who are in Christ. It says dogmatically: 'he who has the Son has life' (1 Jn. 5:12). Indeed, the whole Bible may fairly be described as a divine promise of life, from the first mention of 'the tree of life' in Genesis 3 to the last chapter of the Revelation in which God's redeemed people eat of the tree of life and drink of the water of life freely. Eternal life is a gift 'which God, who never lies, promised ages ago', but has now made known through the preaching of the gospel (cf. verses 9, 10; Tit. 1:2, 3; Rom. 1:1, 2).

This, then, is how Paul introduces himself. He is an apostle of Christ Jesus. His apostleship originated in the will of God and has issued in the proclamation of the gospel of God, namely 'the promise of the life which is in Christ Jesus'.

2. TIMOTHY, PAUL'S BELOVED CHILD (verses 2–8)

To Timothy, my beloved child:

Grace, mercy, and peace from God the Father and Christ Jesus our Lord.

³I thank God whom I serve with a clear conscience, as did my fathers, when I remember you constantly in my prayers. ⁴As I remember your tears, I long night and day to see you, that I may be filled with joy. ⁵I am reminded of your sincere faith, a faith that dwelt first in your grandmother Lois and your mother Eunice and now, I am sure, dwells in you. ⁶Hence I remind you to rekindle the gift of God that is within you through the laying on of my hands; ⁷for God did not give us a spirit of timidity but a spirit of power and love and self-control.

⁸Do not be ashamed then of testifying to our Lord, nor of me his prisoner, but share in suffering for the gospel in the power of God.

Paul calls Timothy here 'my beloved child' and elsewhere 'my beloved and faithful child in the Lord' (1 Cor. 4:17) presumably because he had been the human instrument of Timothy's conversion. Certainly the reason he could describe the Corinthians as 'my beloved children' was 'for I became your father in Christ Jesus through the gospel' (1 Cor. 4:14, 15). We assume, therefore, that when Paul visited Lystra on the first missionary journey 'and there . . . preached the gospel' (Acts 14:6, 7), Timothy both heard and embraced the good news, so that, when Paul re-visited Lystra a few years later on his second missionary journey 'a disciple was there, named Timothy', who had already made such progress in the Christian life that 'he was well spoken of by the brethren at Lystra and Iconium' (Acts 16:1, 2).

To his 'beloved child' Paul now sends his usual greeting of 'grace . . . and peace', though adding in both letters to Timothy 'mercy' as well. We may be sure that this threefold greeting is no mere epistolary convention. For these are pregnant theological words. They tell us much both about man's sorry condition in sin and about God's great love for him all the same. For if grace is God's kindness to the undeserving, mercy is shown to the weak and helpless who cannot help themselves. In the parables of Jesus it was mercy which the good Samaritan showed to the brigands' victim and which the king extended to his servant who was so deeply in debt that he could not pay (Lk. 10:37; Mt. 18:33). And it was mercy which had converted Saul of Tarsus, the old blasphemer and persecutor. 'I received mercy', he had written in his earlier letter to Timothy (1 Tim. 1:13, 16). 'Peace', on the other hand, is reconciliation, the restoration of harmony to lives spoiled by discord. We may perhaps summarize these three blessings of God's love as being grace to the worthless, mercy to the helpless and peace to the restless, while 'God the Father and Christ Jesus our Lord' together constitute the one spring from which this threefold stream flows forth.

There follows a very personal paragraph, in which the apostle assures Timothy that he constantly remembers him. 'I remember you constantly in my prayers,' he says (3). 'I remember your tears' (4). 'I am reminded of your sincere faith' (5). And whenever I remember you, Timothy, 'I thank God' (3).

This last point is significant. It indicates Paul's recognition that it was God who had made Timothy what he was. Timothy was not an apostle like Paul. They used to make this plain when they wrote letters to the churches together, *e.g.* to the Colossians: 'Paul, an apostle of Christ Jesus by the will of God, and Timothy our brother . . .'. Timothy was a Christian brother. He was also a Christian minister, a missionary, and an apostolic delegate. And God had been at work in his life to make him all these things. Directly or indirectly in this paragraph Paul mentions the four major influences which had contributed to the shaping and making of Timothy.

a. His parental upbringing

Paul refers in this paragraph both to his own and to Timothy's ancestry, to his 'forefathers' (3, literally) and to Timothy's mother and grandmother (5). This was right, for every man is to a great extent the product of his inheritance. The most formative influence on each of us has been our parentage and our home. Hence good biographies never begin with their subject, but with his parents, and probably his grandparents as well. True, no man can inherit his parents' faith in the way that he inherits facets of their personality. But a child can be led to faith by his parents' teaching, example and prayers.

Now Timothy had had a godly home. Luke tells us that he was the son of a mixed marriage, in that his father was Greek and his mother Jewish (Acts 16:1). Presumably his father was an unbeliever, but his mother Eunice was a believing Jewess who became a Christian. And before her his grandmother Lois had evidently been converted, for Paul can write of the 'sincere faith' of all three generations (5). Perhaps grandmother, mother and son all owed their conversion to Paul when he brought the gospel to Lystra. Even before their conversion to Christ, however, these godly Jewish women had instructed Timothy out of the Old Testament, so that 'from childhood' he had been 'acquainted with the sacred writings' (3:15). Calvin's rather delightful comment is that Timothy 'was reared in his infancy in such a way that he could suck in godliness along with his mother's milk'.[1]

---

[1] Calvin, p. 292. *Cf.* p. 242 for a similar comment on 1 Tim. 4:6.

Paul could say much the same of himself. He was serving God 'with a clear conscience', as his forefathers had done before him (3). Of course his faith became richer, fuller and deeper when God had revealed Christ to him. Yet it was still substantially the same faith as that of Old Testament believers like Abraham and David, as he had argued in Romans 4, for it was the same God in whom they had all believed. No wonder he had been able to affirm to Felix the procurator: 'I worship the God of my fathers' (Acts 24:14; *cf.* 26:6). We need to remember this when we are witnessing to Jewish people today. A Jew's conversion to Christ is not in any sense an act of disloyalty to his forefathers; it is rather the fulfilment of his forefathers' faith and hope.

Returning to Timothy, the first influence on him was his parental upbringing, and in particular a mother and a grandmother who were sincere believers and who had taught him out of the Scriptures from his childhood. Today also anyone who has been born and bred in a Christian home has received from God a blessing beyond price.

b. His spiritual friendship

After our parents it is our friends who influence us most, especially if they are also in some sense our teachers. And Timothy had in Paul an outstanding teacher-friend.

We have already seen that Paul was Timothy's spiritual 'father'. Having led him to Christ, however, he did not abandon or even forget him. No. He constantly 'remembered' him, as he says repeatedly in this passage. He had also taken him with him on his journeys and trained him as his apprentice. When they had parted on the last occasion, Timothy had been unable to hold back his tears. And now, remembering his tears, Paul longed 'night and day' to see him again, that he might again be 'filled with joy' (4), longed (Bishop Handley Moule renders *epipothōn*) with 'homesick yearning'.[1] Meanwhile, he was praying for him without ceasing (3), and from time to time wrote him letters of counsel and encouragement, like this one.

Such a Christian friendship, including the companionship, the letters and the prayers through which it was expressed, did not

[1] Moule, pp. 40 and 45.

fail to have a powerful moulding effect on young Timothy, strengthening and sustaining him in his Christian life and service.

I thank God for the man who led me to Christ and for the extraordinary devotion with which he nurtured me in the early years of my Christian life. He wrote to me every week for, I think, seven years. He also prayed for me every day. I believe he still does. I can only begin to guess what I owe, under God, to such a faithful friend and pastor.

c. His special endowment

Paul turns now from the indirect means God used to shape Timothy's Christian character (his parents and friends) to a direct gift which God had given him. 'Hence I remind you to rekindle the gift of God that is within you through the laying on of my hands' (6). What this gift of God's grace was, this *charisma*, we do not know with any certainty, for the very good reason that we are not told. We have no liberty to go beyond Scripture. Nevertheless, we can hazard a guess, so long as we recognize its tentative nature. What is clear, both from this verse and from a similar reference in 1 Timothy 4:14, is that the gift was bestowed upon him when Paul and certain 'elders' (probably of the Lystra church) laid their hands on him. Both verses mention the laying-on of hands and seem to refer to what we might call his 'ordination' or 'commissioning'. If we are right so far, then the gift in question was an 'ordination gift', a gift related to his ministry. Paul may indeed be referring to the ministry itself, to which by the laying-on of hands Timothy was set apart. Certainly the offices of pastor and teacher, like those of apostle and prophet, are designated gifts of God's grace (Eph. 4:7, 11). So Dean Alford may be right to say that 'the spiritual gift is that of teaching and ruling the church'.[1] Or the reference may be to the gift of an evangelist, which work Paul will soon urge Timothy to do and so fulfil his ministry (4:5). Or again, since the apostle proceeds at once to refer to the kind of spirit God has given us (7), he may be alluding to a special enduement or anointing of the Spirit which Timothy received at his ordination to equip him

[1] Alford, p. 342, a comment on 1 Tim. 4:14.

for the work to which he had been called. Speaking for myself, I think it is safest to describe Timothy's *charisma* in Alfred Plummer's words as 'the authority and power to be a minister of Christ'.[1] That is, it included both the office and the spiritual equipment needed to fulfil it.

We learn, then, that a man is not only what he owes to his parents, friends and teachers, but what God himself has made him by calling him to some particular ministry and by endowing him with appropriate spiritual resources.

d. His personal discipline

Indeed, all God's gifts—natural and spiritual—need to be developed and used. Our Lord's parables of the talents and the pounds illustrate clearly the duty of service, the reward of faithfulness and the danger of sloth. So Paul tells Timothy in his first letter not to 'neglect' his gift (4:14) and in his second letter rather to 'kindle' or 'rekindle' it (6). The gift is likened to a fire. The Greek verb *anazōpureō*, which occurs nowhere else in the New Testament, does not necessarily imply that Timothy has let the fire die down and must now fan the dying embers into flame again. The prefix *ana* can indicate as much a stirring *up* as a *re*-kindling. It seems, then, that Paul's exhortation is to continue fanning it, to 'stir up that inner fire' (JBP), to keep it alive, even ablaze, presumably by exercising the gift faithfully and by waiting upon God in prayer for its constant renewal.

Having issued this appeal, Paul immediately adds his reason: 'for God did not give us a spirit of timidity but a spirit of power and love and self-control' (7). We have already considered the problems of youth, ill health and temperament with which timid Timothy had to battle. He appears to have been a very shy and sensitive creature, to whom responsibility was an onerous burden. Perhaps he was also fearful of spiritual excesses and extravagances. So Paul is obliged not only to urge him to keep stirring up his gift, but to reassure him that he need not be diffident about exercising it.

Why not? Well, because 'cowardliness has nothing to do with Christianity'.[2] Or, as Paul expresses it, because of the Spirit God

[1] Plummer, p. 314.   [2] Barrett, p. 94.

has given us. Notice that, though a particular spiritual gift was given to 'you', Timothy, the gift of the Spirit himself has been given to *us*, to all of us who are in Christ. And this Spirit God has given to us all is a Spirit not of 'timidity' but of 'power and love and self-control'. Since he is the Spirit of power we may be confident of his enabling as we exercise our ministry. Since he is the Spirit of love we must use God's authority and power in serving others, not in self-assertion or vainglory. And since he is the Spirit of self-control we must use them with seemly reverence and restraint.

So far we have studied what the first seven verses of the letter tell us about these two men, Paul and Timothy, and their making. Paul claims to be Jesus Christ's apostle 'by the will of God', as previously he had said it was 'by the grace of God' that he was what he was (1 Cor. 15:10). And a whole complex of factors had made Timothy what he was—a godly upbringing, Paul's friendship and training, God's gift to him and his own self-discipline in stirring it up.

In principle, it is the same with all God's people. Perhaps the most striking thing is the combination in both Paul and Timothy of divine sovereignty and human responsibility, those two facts of revelation and of experience which we find it difficult to reconcile and impossible to systematize into a tidy doctrine.

Paul could write of God's will and assert that God's grace had made him what he was. But then he would at once add: 'and his grace toward me was not in vain. On the contrary, I worked harder than any of them, though it was not I, but the grace of God which is with me' (1 Cor. 15:10). That is, he added his labour to God's grace, although, to be sure, it was God's grace which inspired his labour.

Timothy was similar. His mother and grandmother could teach him out of the Scriptures and lead him towards conversion. Paul could actually bring him to Christ, befriend him, pray for him, write to him, train and exhort him. And God could give him a special gift at his ordination. But still Timothy must himself stir up the divine gift within him. He must add his own self-discipline to God's gifts.

We are no different. However much (or little) we may have

received from God, either directly in natural and spiritual endowment or indirectly through parents, friends and teachers, we must still apply ourselves in active self-discipline to co-operate with God's grace, to keep fanning the inner fire into flame. Otherwise, we shall never be the men and women God wants us to be, or fulfil the ministry he has given us to exercise.

Paul now turns from the varied factors which had contributed to the making of Timothy to the truth of the gospel and to Timothy's responsibility in relation to the gospel. Before he defines the gospel, he begs Timothy not to be ashamed of it (8). Suffering rather than shame is to characterize Timothy's ministry. He may be young, frail, timid and weak. He may shrink from the tasks to which he is being called. But God has moulded and gifted him for his ministry. So he must not be ashamed or afraid to exercise it.

This means, to begin with, that Timothy must 'not be ashamed' of Christ, 'of testifying to our Lord'. Every Christian is Christ's witness, and Christian testimony is essentially testimony to or about Christ (*cf.* Jn. 15:26, 27; Acts 1:8). So every Christian must be ready and willing, if necessary, to be a 'fool for Christ's sake' (1 Cor. 4:10); he need not be prepared to be a fool for any-one else's!

If Timothy must not be ashamed of the Lord, he must not be ashamed of Paul either. For it is possible to be proud of Christ, but ashamed of his people and embarrassed to be associated with them. It seems that when Paul was re-arrested and put in chains, nearly all his former supporters forsook him (15). He now begs Timothy not to follow suit. He may be the emperor's prisoner in the eyes of men; he is the Lord's prisoner in reality, his willing captive, and held in prison by man only by Christ's permission and for Christ's sake.[1]

Timothy must also not be ashamed of the gospel, but rather

---

[1] During his earlier house arrest in Rome Paul called himself a (or the) 'prisoner of Christ Jesus' in Eph. 3:1 and Phm. 1, 9, just as here he is 'his prisoner', while in Eph. 4:1 the expression he used was 'the prisoner in the Lord' (*en kuriō*), meaning perhaps that he had been imprisoned because of his union with Christ.

take his share of suffering for it. Weak as he was in himself, he could be fortified by the power of God to endure it. For endure suffering he must, since the gospel of Christ crucified, folly to some and a stumbling-block to others (1 Cor. 1:23), always arouses opposition. And opposing the message, men naturally oppose its messengers, who thus 'suffer with the suffering gospel'.[1]

These are still the three main ways in which Christian people, like Timothy, are tempted to feel ashamed: now of the *name* of Christ, to whom we are called to witness, now of the *people* of Christ, to whom we also belong if we belong to him, and now of the *gospel* of Christ, which is entrusted to us to spread.

The temptation is strong and insidious. If Timothy had not felt it, Paul would not have exhorted him in these terms. If Paul himself had never felt it, it would have been unnecessary for him some years previously to assert with such vehemence, 'For I am not ashamed of the gospel: it is the power of God for salvation to everyone who has faith' (Rom. 1:16). Indeed, if this were not a temptation common to man, the Lord Jesus would not have needed to issue the solemn warning, 'For whoever is ashamed of me and of my words in this adulterous and sinful generation, of him will the Son of man also be ashamed, when he comes in the glory of his Father with the holy angels' (Mk. 8:38). We are all more sensitive to public opinion than we like to admit, and tend to bow down too readily before its pressure, like reeds shaken by the wind.

Paul now enlarges on the gospel of which Timothy is not to be ashamed, and for which he must take his share of suffering. He begins by sketching its main features (9, 10) and then summarizes our responsibility in relation to it (11–18). This then is the double theme of the rest of the chapter: God's gospel and our duty.

[1] Moule, pp. 45, 72.

3. GOD'S GOSPEL (verses 9, 10)

... who saved us and called us with a holy calling, not in virtue of our works but in virtue of his own purpose and the grace which he gave us in Christ Jesus ages ago, [10] and now has manifested through the appearing of our Saviour Christ Jesus, who abolished death and brought life and immortality to light through the gospel.

It is striking to hear Paul pass at once from a reference to 'the gospel' to the central affirmation 'God . . . saved us'. For it is really impossible to speak of the gospel without going on in the same breath to speak of salvation. The gospel is precisely this, good news of salvation, or good news 'of our Saviour Christ Jesus' (10). Ever since the glad tidings of great joy were first announced on Christmas Day in terms of the birth of 'a Saviour who is Christ the Lord' (Lk. 2:10, 11), the followers of Jesus have recognized its essential content. Paul himself never wavered. In Pisidian Antioch during the first missionary journey he referred to his gospel as 'the message of this salvation'. In Philippi during the second missionary journey he and his companions were described as 'servants of the Most High God, who proclaimed to you the way of salvation'. And writing to the Ephesians from Rome he called the word of truth 'the gospel of your salvation' (Acts 13:26; 16:17; Eph. 1:13).

So here, as Paul writes about the gospel, the terminology which he has made familiar recurs, namely that we are saved in Christ Jesus by God's purpose, grace and call, and not by our own works. For he is expounding the same gospel in his last letter (2 Timothy) as he expounded in his first (Galatians). His gospel has not changed with the passing years. There is only one gospel of salvation. And although both words 'gospel' and 'salvation' need today to be translated into terms meaningful to modern man, we have no liberty to alter the substance of our message. As we come to look more closely at the concise statement of God's gospel which he makes in these verses, we shall see that he indicates its character (what it is), its source (where it comes from) and its ground (on what it rests).

a. The character of salvation

We need to bring together the three clauses which assert that he 'saved us', he 'called us with a holy calling' and he 'brought life and immortality to light'. For these make it plain that salvation is far more than forgiveness. The God who 'saved' us also and simultaneously 'called us with a holy calling', *i.e.* 'called us to be holy' (JB). The Christian calling is a holy calling. When God calls a man to himself, he calls him to holiness also. Paul has laid much emphasis on this in his earlier letters. 'God has not called us for uncleanness, but in holiness.' For all of us are 'called to be saints', called to live as the holy, the separated people of God (1 Thes. 4:7; 1 Cor. 1:2). But if holiness is an integral part of God's plan of salvation, so is the 'immortality' of which he writes in the following verse (10). Indeed, 'forgiveness', 'holiness' and 'immortality' are all three aspects of God's great 'salvation'.

The term 'salvation' urgently needs to be rescued from the mean and meagre concepts to which we tend to degrade it. 'Salvation' is a majestic word, denoting that comprehensive purpose of God by which he justifies, sanctifies and glorifies his people: first, pardoning our offences and accepting us as righteous in his sight through Christ, then progressively transforming us by his Spirit into the image of his Son, until finally we become like Christ in heaven, with new bodies in a new world. We must not minimize the greatness of 'such a great salvation' (Heb. 2:3).

b. The source of salvation

Where does such a great salvation come from? Paul answers, 'not in virtue of our works but in virtue of his own purpose and the grace which he gave us in Christ ages ago' (9). If we would trace the river of salvation to its source, we must look right back beyond time to a past eternity. The apostle's actual words are 'before eternal times',[1] an expression variously rendered 'before the world began' (AV), 'before time began' (JBP) and 'from all eternity' (NEB).

In order to put beyond question the truth that God's pre-

---

[1] *pro chronōn aiōniōn.* The same expression occurs in Titus 1:2 with reference to God's promise of life. *Cf.* Rom. 16:25.

destination and election belong to eternity and not to time, Paul uses an aorist participle to indicate that God actually gave us something (*dotheisan*) from all eternity in Christ. What he gave us was 'his own purpose and grace', a hendiadys for 'his own purpose of grace'. His saving purpose was not arbitrary, but gracious.[1] It is plain, therefore, that the source of our salvation is not our own works. For God gave us his own purpose of grace in Christ before we did any good works, before we were born and could do any good works, indeed before history, before time, in eternity.

We have to confess that the doctrine of election is difficult to finite minds. But it is incontrovertibly a biblical doctrine. It emphasizes that salvation is due to God's grace alone, not to man's merit; not to our works performed in time, but to God's purpose conceived in eternity, 'that purpose', as Bishop Ellicott expressed it, 'which was suggested by nothing outward, but arose only from the innermost depths of the divine *eudokia*'.[2] Or, in E. K. Simpson's words, 'the Lord's choices have their unfathomable grounds, but they are not founded on the innate eligibility of the chosen'.[3] Thus understood, God's purpose of election is bound to be mysterious to men, for we cannot aspire to an understanding of the secret thoughts and decisions of the mind of God. However, the doctrine of election is never introduced in Scripture either to arouse or to baffle our carnal curiosity, but always for a practical purpose. On the one hand, it engenders deep humility and gratitude, for it excludes all boasting. On the other, it brings both peace and assurance, for nothing can quieten our fears for our own stability like the knowledge that our safety depends ultimately not on ourselves but on God's own purpose of grace.

c. The ground of salvation

Our salvation rests firmly grounded upon the historical work performed by Jesus Christ at his first appearing. For though

---

[1] See Rom. 8:28; 9:11 and Eph. 1:11 for other examples of God's predestinating, saving 'purpose' (*prothesis*).

[2] Ellicott, p. 115; *eudokia* means 'good pleasure'.

[3] Simpson, p. 125.

God 'gave' us his grace in Christ Jesus 'before eternal times', he 'manifested' it in time, 'now', through the appearing of the same Christ Jesus, our Saviour. Both divine stages were in and through Jesus Christ, but the giving was eternal and secret, while the manifesting was historical and public.

What, then, did Christ do when he appeared and proceeded to manifest God's eternal purpose of grace? To this Paul gives in verse 10 a double answer. First, Jesus Christ 'abolished death'. Secondly, he 'brought life and immortality to light through the gospel'.

First, Christ abolished death.

'Death' is, in fact, the one word which summarizes our human predicament as a result of sin. For death is the 'wage' sin pays, its grim penalty (Rom. 6:23). And this is true of each form which death takes. For Scripture speaks of death in three ways. There is physical death, the separation of the soul from the body. There is spiritual death, the separation of the soul from God. And there is eternal death, the separation of both soul and body from God for ever. All are due to sin; they are sin's terrible though just reward.

But Jesus Christ 'abolished' death. This cannot mean that he eliminated it, as we know from our everyday experience. Sinners are still 'dead through the trespasses and sins' in which they walk (Eph. 2:1, 2) until God makes them alive in Christ. All human beings die physically and will continue to do so, with the exception of the generation who are alive when Christ returns in glory. And some are going to die 'the second death', which is one of the fearful expressions used in the book of Revelation for hell (*e.g.* Rev. 20:14; 21:8). Indeed, Paul has written previously that the final abolition of death still lies in the future, as the last enemy of God to be destroyed (1 Cor. 15:26). Not until the return of Christ and the resurrection of the dead shall we be able to shout with joy 'Death is swallowed up in victory' (1 Cor. 15:54; *cf.* Rev. 21:4).

What is triumphantly asserted in this verse by Paul is that at his first appearing Christ decisively 'defeated' or 'overthrew' death. The Greek verb *katargeō* is not in itself conclusive, for it can be used with a variety of meanings, which must be determined by the context. Nevertheless, its first and foremost meaning is 'make ineffective, powerless, idle' or 'nullify' (AG). So Paul can liken death to a scorpion whose sting has been drawn and to a military commander whose army has been defeated, and can cry out with defiance: 'O death, where is thy victory? O death, where is thy sting?' (1 Cor. 15:55). For Christ 'has broken the power of death' (AG, NEB).

It is surely significant that this same verb *katargeō* is used in the New Testament with reference to the devil and to our fallen nature as well as to death (Heb. 2:14; Rom. 6:6). Neither the devil, nor our fallen nature, nor death has been annihilated. But by the power of Christ the tyranny of each has been broken, so that if we are in Christ we can be set free.

Consider in particular how Christ has 'abolished' or 'nullified' death.

Physical death is no longer the grim ogre it once seemed to us and still seems to many whom Christ has not yet liberated. 'Through fear of death' they are 'subject to lifelong bondage' (Heb. 2:15). But for Christian believers death is simply 'falling asleep' in Christ. It is, in fact, a positive 'gain', because it is the gateway to being 'with Christ' which is 'far better'. It is one of the possessions which become 'ours' when we are Christ's (1 Thes. 4:14, 15; Phil. 1:21, 23; 1 Cor. 3:22, 23). It has been rendered so innocuous that Jesus could even state that the believer, though he dies, 'shall never die' (Jn. 11:25, 26). What is absolutely certain is that death will never be able to separate us from God's love in Christ (Rom. 8:38, 39).

Spiritual death has, for Christian believers, given place to that eternal life which is communion with God begun on earth and perfected in heaven. Further, those who are in Christ will 'not be hurt by the second death', for they have already passed out of death into life (Rev. 2:11; Jn. 5:24; 1 Jn. 3:14).

Secondly, Christ brought life and immortality to light through the gospel.

This is the positive counterpart. It is by his death and resurrection that Christ abolished death. It is through the gospel that he now reveals what he has done, and offers men the life and immortality which he has won for them. Whether we should distinguish between the words 'life' and 'immortality' is not clear. They may be synonymous, the second word defining the first. That is, the kind of life Christ has secured for us, and now discloses and offers through the gospel is eternal life, a life that is immortal and incorruptible. Only God possesses immortality in himself. But Christ gives it to men. Even our bodies after the resurrection will share in this immortality (1 Cor. 15:42, 52–54). So will the inheritance which we shall receive (1 Pet. 1:4). On the other hand, as C. K. Barrett writes: 'possibly "life" refers to the new life made available in this world, "immortality" to its prolongation after death'.[1] Whichever way we take the words, both are 'revealed' or 'brought to light' through the gospel. There are many hints in Old Testament Scripture about a life after death, and a few bright flashes of faith, but on the whole the Old Testament revelation was what Bishop Moule called a 'comparative dusk'.[2] Now, however, the gospel has thrown floods of light upon the offer of immortal life through Christ's conquest of death.

In order to appreciate the full force of this Christian affirmation, we need to call to mind who it is who is making it. Who is this who writes so confidently about life and death, about the abolition of death and the revelation of life? It is one who is facing the prospect of imminent death himself. Any day now he expects to receive the death sentence. Already the final summons is ringing in his ears. Already he can see in his imagination the flash of the executioner's sword. And yet, in the very presence of death, he can shout aloud: 'Christ has abolished death'. This is Christian faith triumphant!

How one longs for the contemporary church to recover its lost certainty about the victory of Jesus Christ and to declare this good news to a world for whom death is the great unmentionable. *The Observer* magazine devoted a whole issue to death in October 1968 and commented: 'Far from being prepared for death, modern society has made the very word almost unmentionable . . . we have brought all our talents into use to avoid the prospect of dying—and when the time comes we may react with anything from excessive triviality to total despair.'

One of the most searching tests to apply to any religion concerns its attitude to death. And measured by this test much so-called Christianity is found wanting with its black clothes, its mournful chants and its requiem masses. Of course dying can be

[1] Barrett, p. 95.   [2] Moule, p. 50.

very unpleasant, and bereavement can bring bitter sorrow. But death itself has been overthrown, and 'blessed are the dead who die in the Lord' (Rev. 14:13). The proper epitaph to write for a Christian believer is not a dismal and uncertain petition, 'R.I.P.' (*requiescat in pace*, 'may he rest in peace'), but a joyful and certain affirmation 'C.A.D.' ('Christ abolished death') or—if you prefer the classical languages—its Greek or Latin equivalent!

Such, then, is the salvation which is offered us in the gospel and which is ours in Christ. Its *character* is man's re-creation and transformation into the holiness of Christ here and hereafter. Its *source* is God's eternal purpose of grace. Its *ground* is Christ's historical appearing and abolition of death.

Putting these great truths together, we seem to detect five stages by which God's saving purpose unfolds. The first is the eternal gift to us in Christ of his grace. The second is the historical appearing of Christ to abolish death by his death and resurrection. The third is the personal call of God to sinners through the preaching of the gospel. The fourth is the moral sanctification of believers by the Holy Spirit. And the fifth is the final heavenly perfection in which the holy calling is consummated.

The sweep of God's purpose of grace is majestic indeed, as Paul traces it from a past eternity through a historical outworking in Jesus Christ and in the Christian to an ultimate destiny with Christ and like Christ in a future immortality. Is it not truly wonderful that, although Paul's body is confined within the narrow limits of an underground cell, his heart and mind can thus soar into eternity?

4. OUR DUTY IN RELATION TO GOD'S GOSPEL
(verses 11–18)

For this gospel I was appointed a preacher and apostle and teacher, [12] *and therefore I suffer as I do. But I am not ashamed, for I know whom I have believed, and I am sure that he is able to guard until that Day what has been entrusted to me.* [13] *Follow the pattern of the sound words which you have heard from me, in the faith and love which are in Christ Jesus;* [14] *guard the truth that has been entrusted to you by the Holy Spirit who dwells within us.*

[15] *You are aware that all who are in Asia turned away from me, and among them Phygelus and Hermogenes.* [16] *May the Lord grant mercy to the household of Onesiphorus, for he often refreshed me; he was not ashamed of my chains,* [17] *but when he arrived in Rome he searched for me eagerly and found me*—[18] *may the Lord grant him to find mercy from the Lord on that Day—and you well know all the service he rendered at Ephesus.*

If we were to ask Paul what man's first duty is in relation to the gospel, he would of course say to receive it and live by it. But his concern here is not with the unbeliever's duty, but with the duty of a Christian towards the gospel after he has himself embraced it. In answer to this question Paul gives three answers.

a. Our duty to communicate the gospel (verse 11)

If the 'life and immortality' which Christ achieved are 'brought . . . to light through the gospel', then of course it is imperative that we should proclaim the gospel. So Paul continues: 'For this gospel I was appointed a preacher and apostle and teacher.' The same combination of words occurs in 1 Timothy 2:7, and in both Paul uses the emphatic *egō*, no doubt to express his 'sense of personal wonder'[1] that he should have been given this privilege.

Perhaps we can relate the three offices of 'apostle', 'preacher' and 'teacher' by saying that the apostles formulated the gospel, preachers proclaim it like heralds, and teachers instruct people systematically in its doctrines and in its ethical implications.

There are no apostles of Christ today. We have already seen how restricted is the New Testament use of this term. The gospel was formulated by the apostles and has now been bequeathed by them to the church. It is found in its definitive form in the New Testament. This apostolic New Testament faith is regulative for the church of every age and place. The church is 'built upon the foundation of the apostles and prophets' (Eph. 2:20). There is no other gospel. There can be no new gospel.

Although there are no apostles of Christ today, there are certainly preachers and teachers, men and women called by God to devote themselves to the work of preaching and teaching.

[1] Guthrie, p. 73.

Notice that what they are called both to preach and to teach is the gospel. It is fashionable in theological circles to distinguish sharply between the *kērygma* (what was preached) and the *didachē* (what was taught), the *kērygma* being essentially the good news of Christ crucified and risen, with the summons to repent and believe, the *didachē* being largely ethical instruction to converts. The distinction is useful, but can be overpressed. It is safe only if we remember how much they overlapped. There was a lot of *didachē* in the *kērygma* and a lot of *kērygma* in the *didachē*. And, moreover, both concerned the gospel, for the *kērygma* was the proclamation of its essence, while the *didachē* included the great doctrines which undergird it as well as the moral behaviour which follows from it.

The reference to 'witness' in verse 8, which we have already considered, adds a fourth word to this list. It reminds us that, although there are no apostles today, and although only some are called to the ministry of preaching and teaching, every Christian believer is to be a witness and to testify to Jesus Christ out of his own personal experience.

b. Our duty to suffer for the gospel (verse 12a)

Paul has already summoned Timothy not to be ashamed but to take his share of suffering for the gospel (8), and he will enlarge on this theme in the second chapter of his letter. But now he emphasizes that he is not asking from Timothy something he is not prepared to experience himself: '. . . and therefore I suffer as I do. But I am not ashamed . . .' What is the reason for this link between suffering and the gospel? What is there about the gospel which men hate and oppose, and on account of which those who preach it have to suffer?

Just this: God saves sinners in virtue of his own purpose and grace, and not in virtue of their good works (9). It is the undeserved freeness of the gospel which offends. The 'natural' or unregenerate man hates to have to admit the gravity of his sin and guilt, his complete helplessness to save himself, the indispensable necessity of God's grace and Christ's sinbearing death to save him, and therefore his inescapable indebtedness to the cross. This is what Paul meant by 'the stumbling block of the cross'.

Many preachers succumb to the temptation to mute it. They preach man and his merit instead of Christ and his cross, and they substitute the one for the other 'in order that they may not be persecuted for the cross of Christ' (Gal. 6:12; *cf.* 5:11). No man can preach Christ crucified with faithfulness and escape opposition, even persecution.

c. Our duty to guard the gospel (verses 12b–18)

Leaving aside for the moment the second part of verse 12, we come to Paul's double exhortation to Timothy in the next two verses: 'Follow the pattern of the sound words which you have heard from me' (13); 'Guard the truth that has been entrusted to you' (14). Here Paul refers to the gospel, the apostolic faith, by two expressions. It is both a pattern of sound words (13) and a precious deposit (14).

'Sound' words are 'healthy' words, the Greek expression being used in the Gospels of people whom Jesus healed. Previously they had been maimed or diseased; now they were well or 'whole'. So the Christian faith is 'the sound teaching' (4:3), consisting of 'sound words', because it is not maimed or diseased but 'whole'. It is what Paul had previously called 'the whole counsel of God' (Acts 20:27).

Further, these 'sound words' had been given by Paul to Timothy in a 'pattern'. Here the Greek word is *hypotypōsis*. NEB translates it 'outline', and Dr. Guthrie says it 'means an outline sketch such as an architect might make before getting down to the detailed plans of a building'.[1] In this case Paul is implying that Timothy must amplify, expound and apply the apostle's teaching. The context, especially the parallel with the next verse, seems to me to make this an unlikely explanation. The only other occurrence of *hypotypōsis* in the New Testament is in Paul's first letter to Timothy where he describes himself, the object of Christ's amazing mercy and perfect patience, as 'an *example* to those who were to believe in him' (1:16). Arndt and Gingrich, who give 'model' or 'example' as the usual translation, suggest that it is used 'rather in the sense *prototype*' in 1 Timothy 1:16 and 'rather in the sense *standard*' in 2 Timothy 1:13. In this case Paul is

[1] Guthrie, p. 132.

commanding Timothy to keep before him as his standard of sound words, or 'as a model of sound teaching' (NEB mg.) what he had heard from the apostle. This certainly suits the general teaching of the letter and faithfully reflects the emphasis of the sentence on the first word 'model' or 'standard'.

So Paul's teaching is to be Timothy's guide or rule. He is not to depart from it. He is to follow it, better to hold it fast (*eche*). And he must do so 'in the faith and love which are in Christ Jesus'. That is, Paul is concerned not just with *what* Timothy is to do, but with *how* he does it. His personal doctrinal convictions and his instruction of others, as he grips hold of Paul's teaching, are to be characterized by faith and love. He is to seek these qualities from Christ, a sincere belief and a tender charity.

The apostolic faith is not only 'a standard of sound words'; it is also 'the good deposit' (*hē kalē parathēkē*). These are the words which the AV renders 'that good thing which was committed unto thee', the RSV 'the truth that has been entrusted to you', and the NEB 'the treasure put into your charge'. For the gospel is a treasure—a good, noble and precious treasure—deposited for safe keeping with the church. Christ had entrusted it to Paul, and Paul now entrusts it to Timothy.

Timothy is to 'guard' it. Paul has addressed precisely the same appeal to him at the end of his first letter (6:20), except that now he calls it the 'good', literally the 'beautiful', deposit. The verb (*phylassō*) means to guard something 'so that it is not lost or damaged' (AG). It is used of guarding a palace against marauders and possessions against thieves (Lk. 11:21; Acts 22:20). There were heretics abroad, bent on corrupting the gospel and so robbing the church of the priceless treasure which had been entrusted to it. Timothy must be on the watch.

And he must guard the gospel all the more tenaciously because of what had happened in and around Ephesus (the capital of the Roman province of Asia) where Timothy was (15). The aorist tense of the verb 'turned away from me' seems to refer to some particular event. The most likely allusion is to the moment of the apostle's re-arrest. The churches of Asia, where he had laboured for several years, had depended heavily upon him. Perhaps his arrest seemed to them to indicate that the Christian cause was now lost. Perhaps they reacted by repudiating and disowning him.

We know nothing of Phygelus and Hermogenes, but their mention suggests they were the ringleaders. In any case Paul saw the turning away of the Asian churches as more than a personal desertion; it was a disavowal of his apostolic authority. It must have seemed particularly tragic, because a few years previously, during Paul's two and a half years' residence in Ephesus, Luke says that 'all the residents of Asia' heard the word of the Lord and many believed (Acts 19:10). Now 'all in Asia' had turned away from him. The great awakening had been followed by a great defection. 'To every eye but that of faith it must have appeared just then as if the gospel were on the eve of extinction.'[1]

The one bright exception appears to have been a man called Onesiphorus, who had often entertained Paul in his home (literally 'refreshed' him, verse 16), and had rendered him other, unspecified service in Ephesus (18). He had thus been true to the meaning of his name, 'a bringer of profit'. In addition, he had not been ashamed of Paul's chains (16), which seems to mean both that he did not repudiate him at the time of his arrest and that he then followed him, even accompanied him, to Rome, and then searched diligently for him until he found him in his dungeon. Paul had good reason to be grateful for this faithful and courageous friend. It is not surprising, therefore, that he twice utters a prayer (16, 18), first for his household ('may the Lord grant mercy to the household of Onesiphorus') and then for Onesiphorus himself ('may the Lord grant him to find mercy from the Lord on that Day').

Various commentators, especially Roman Catholics, have argued from the references to the household of Onesiphorus (mentioned again in 4:19) and to 'that Day' that Onesiphorus himself was now dead, and that we have therefore in verse 18 a petition for the departed. This is an entirely gratuitous assumption, however. The fact that Paul keeps distinct his allusions to Onesiphorus on the one hand and to his household on the other could equally well mean that they were separated from each other by distance as by death, Onesiphorus being still in Rome, while his family were at home in Ephesus. 'I take it to be a prayer for them separately, the man and his family,' writes Bishop Handley Moule, 'because they were for the time separated from one

[1] Moule, p. 16.

another by lands and seas . . . There is no need at all to assume
that Onesiphorus had died. Separation from his family by a
journey quite satisfies the language of the passage.'[1]

At all events, everybody in Asia, as Timothy was keenly
aware, had turned away from the apostle, with the exception of
loyal Onesiphorus and his family. It was in such a situation of
almost universal apostasy that Timothy was to 'guard the good
deposit', to 'hold firm the standard of sound words', that is to
say, to preserve the gospel unsullied and unalloyed. It would
have been a heavy responsibility for any man, let alone a man
of Timothy's temperament. How then could he stand firm?

The apostle gives Timothy the reassurance he needs. He cannot
hope to guard the gospel-treasure by himself; he can do it only
'by the Holy Spirit who dwells within us' (14b). The same truth
is taught in the second part of verse 12, which so far we have not
considered. Most Christians are familiar with the AV rendering
'for I know whom I have believed, and am persuaded that he is
able to keep that which I have committed unto him against that
day'. These words are true, for many biblical passages confirm
them, and linguistically speaking, they are accurately translated.
But the context makes another interpretation more probable.
The AV words 'that which I have committed unto him' are a
rendering of 'my deposit' (*tēn parathēkēn mou*). Indeed, both the
verb ('guard') and the noun ('deposit') are precisely the same in
verse 12 as in verse 14 and in 1 Timothy 6:20. The presumption is
therefore that 'my deposit' is not what I have committed to him
(my soul or myself, as in 1 Pet. 4:19) but what he has committed to me (the gospel).

The sense, then, is this. The deposit is 'mine', Paul could say,
because Christ had committed it to him. Yet Paul was persuaded
that Christ would himself keep it safe 'until that Day' when he
would have to give an account of his stewardship. What was the
ground of his confidence? Just this: 'I know him.' Paul knew
Christ in whom he had put his trust and was convinced of his
ability to keep the deposit safe: 'I know whom I have believed,
and I am sure that he is able to guard until that Day what has
been entrusted to me' (12). He has entrusted it to me, it is true;
but he will take care of it himself. And now that Paul is entrusting

[1] Moule, pp. 67, 68.

it to Timothy, Timothy can be sustained by the same assurance.

There is great encouragement here. Ultimately, it is God himself who is the guarantor of the gospel. It is his responsibility to preserve it. 'On no other ground would the work of preaching be for a moment endurable.'[1] We may see the evangelical faith, the faith of the gospel, everywhere spoken against, and the apostolic message of the New Testament ridiculed. We may have to watch an increasing apostasy in the church, as our generation abandons the faith of its fathers. Do not be afraid! God will never allow the light of the gospel to be finally extinguished. True, he has committed it to us, frail and fallible creatures. He has placed his treasure in brittle, earthenware vessels. And we must play our part in guarding and defending the truth. Nevertheless, in entrusting the deposit to our hands, he has not taken his own hands off it. He is himself its final guardian, and *he* will preserve the truth which he has committed to the church. We know this because we know him in whom we have trusted and continue to trust.

We have seen that the gospel is good news of salvation, promised from eternity, secured by Christ in time, offered to faith.

Our first duty is to *communicate* this gospel, to use old ways and seek fresh ways of making it known throughout the whole world.

If we do so, we shall undoubtedly *suffer* for it, for the authentic gospel has never been popular. It humbles the sinner too much.

And when we are called to suffer for the gospel, we are tempted to trim it, to eliminate those elements which give offence and cause opposition, to mute the notes which jar on sensitive modern ears.

But we must resist the temptation. For, above all, we are called to *guard* the gospel, keeping it pure whatever the cost, and preserving it against every corruption.

Guard it faithfully. Spread it actively. Suffer for it bravely. This is our threefold duty vis-à-vis the gospel of God as expounded in this first chapter.

[1] Barrett, p. 97.

Chapter 2

THE CHARGE TO SUFFER FOR THE GOSPEL

1. HANDING ON THE TRUTH (verses 1, 2)

You then, my son, be strong in the grace that is in Christ Jesus, ²and what you have heard from me before many witnesses entrust to faithful men who will be able to teach others also.

THE first chapter ended with Paul's sorrowful reference to the widespread defection among Christians in the Roman province of Asia (1:15). Onesiphorus and his household seem to have been the outstanding exception. Now Paul urges Timothy that he too, in the midst of the general landslide, must stand his ground. It is the first of several similar exhortations in the letter, beginning *su oun* or *su de* meaning 'you therefore' or 'but you', which summon Timothy to resist the prevailing mood. Timothy had been called to responsible leadership in the church not only in spite of his natural diffidence but in the very area where the apostle's authority was being repudiated. It is as if Paul says to him: 'Never mind what other people may be thinking or saying or doing. Never mind how weak and shy you yourself may feel. As for you, Timothy, be strong!'

Of course if his exhortation had stopped there, it would have been futile, even absurd. He might as well have told a snail to be quick or a horse to fly as command a man as timid as Timothy to be strong. But Paul's call to fortitude is Christian not stoical. It is not a summons to Timothy to be strong in himself—to set his jaw and grit his teeth—but to 'be inwardly strengthened'[1] by means of 'the grace that is in Christ Jesus'. NEB expands the

---

[1] I take the verb as being 'simply passive' (Ellicott, p. 121), although it might be the middle voice 'strengthen yourself inwardly'. The same verb occurs passively in Eph. 6:10 and actively in Phil. 4:13 and 2 Tim. 4:17.

sentence thus: 'Take strength from the grace of God which is ours in Christ Jesus.' Timothy is to find his resources for ministry not in his own nature but in Christ's grace. It is not only for salvation that we are dependent on grace (1:9), but for service also.

Paul proceeds to indicate the kind of ministry for which Timothy will need to strengthen himself by Christ's grace. So far he has been exhorted to hold the faith and guard the deposit (1:13, 14). He is to do more than preserve the truth, however; he is also to pass it on. If the disloyalty of the Asian church made it imperative that Timothy should guard the truth with loyalty, the approaching death of the apostle made it equally imperative that Timothy should make arrangements for the handing down of the truth intact to the next generation. In this transmission of truth from hand to hand Paul envisages four stages.

First, the faith has been entrusted to Paul by Christ. This is why he has called it 'my deposit' (1:12). It is his by deposit, not by invention. As an apostle of Jesus Christ he insists that his gospel is 'not man's gospel', whether his own composition or somebody else's. Nor is he relying purely on human tradition. On the contrary, he could write: 'I did not receive it from man, nor was I taught it, but it came through a revelation of Jesus Christ' (Gal. 1:11, 12).

Secondly, what has been entrusted to Paul by Christ Paul in his turn has entrusted to Timothy. So 'my deposit' becomes virtually 'your deposit', and 'what has been entrusted to me' (1:12) is now 'the truth that has been entrusted to you' (1:14). This deposit consists of certain 'sound words' which Timothy has heard from Paul's own lips. The exact expression 'you have heard from me' (1:13 *par' emou ēkousas*) is repeated in 2:2, though now with the addition that Timothy has heard it 'before many witnesses'. The aorist tense would seem to refer not to a single public occasion on which Timothy heard the apostle's teaching—such as his baptism or ordination—but rather to the totality of his instruction over the years. And the reference to the many witnesses shows that the apostolic faith was not a secret tradition handed on privately to Timothy (such as the Gnostics were claiming), whose authenticity there was no means of testing, but a public instruction, whose truth was guaranteed by the many witnesses who had heard it and who could therefore check Timothy's teaching against the apostle's.

This statement of Paul's became important in the following century when Gnosticism had grown and spread. For example, in chapter 25 of his *Prescriptions against Heretics* (*c.* AD 200) Tertullian of Carthage was particularly writing against Gnostics who claimed both to have had private revelations of their own and to possess secret traditions handed down from the apostles. He would not allow that the apostles had 'entrusted some things openly to all and some things secretly to a few'. For (he argued) in appealing to Timothy to guard the deposit 'there is no hinting at a hidden doctrine, but a command not to admit any but the teaching which he had heard from Paul himself and (I think) openly—"before many witnesses" as he says'.[1]

Thirdly, what Timothy has heard from Paul he is now to 'entrust to faithful men', of whom there are evidently some left among the many deserters of Asia. The men Paul has in mind must be primarily ministers of the word, whose chief function is to teach, Christian elders whose responsibility it would be— like the Jewish elders of the synagogue—to preserve the tradition. Such Christian elders are 'God's stewards', as Paul has recently written to Titus (1:7), because both God's household and God's truth are committed to their trust. And the fundamental requirement in stewards is trustworthiness (1 Cor. 4:1, 2). They must be 'faithful men'.

Fourthly, such men must be the sort of men who (as the relative *hoitines* should be translated) 'will be able to teach others also'. The ability or competence which Timothy must look for in such men will consist partly in their integrity or faithfulness of character already mentioned and partly in their facility for teaching. They must be *didaktikoi*, 'apt teachers', a word Paul has used of candidates for the ministry in 1 Timothy 3:2 and will use again later in this chapter (2:24).

Here, then, are the four stages in the handing on of the truth, which Paul envisages: from Christ to Paul, from Paul to Timothy, from Timothy to 'faithful men', and from 'faithful men' to 'others also'. This is the true 'apostolic succession'. Certainly

[1] *Early Latin Theology*, edited by S. L. Greenslade (Vol. V of the SCM Library of Christian Classics, 1956), p. 47.

it would involve men, a line of 'faithful men' at that, but the succession from the apostles is to be more in the message itself than in the men who teach it. It is to be a succession of apostolic tradition rather than of apostolic ministry, authority or order, a transmission of the apostles' doctrine handed down unchanged from the apostles to subsequent generations, and passed from hand to hand like the Olympic torch. This apostolic tradition, 'the good deposit', is now to be found in the New Testament. Speaking ideally, 'Scripture' and 'tradition' should be interchangeable terms, for what the church hands down from generation to generation should be the biblical faith, no more and no less. And the biblical faith is the apostolic faith.

In the rest of this second chapter of his letter Paul enlarges on the teaching ministry to which Timothy has been called. He illustrates it by using six vivid metaphors. The first three are already favourite images with Paul—the soldier, the athlete and the farmer. He has made use of them several times in former letters to enforce a wide variety of truths. Here they all emphasize that Timothy's work will be strenuous, involving both labour and suffering.

2. METAPHOR I: THE DEDICATED SOLDIER (verses 3, 4)

Share in suffering as a good soldier of Christ Jesus. ⁴*No soldier on service gets entangled in civilian pursuits, since his aim is to satisfy the one who enlisted him.*

Paul's prison experiences had given him ample opportunity to watch Roman soldiers and to meditate on the parallels between the soldier and the Christian. In earlier letters he has referred to the warfare with principalities and powers in which the Christian soldier is engaged, the armour which he must put on and the weapons which he must use (Eph. 6:10 ff.; 1 Tim. 1:18; 6:12; 2 Cor. 6:7; 10:3-5; *cf.* Rom. 6:13, 14). But here the 'good soldier of Christ Jesus' is so called because he is a dedicated man, who shows his dedication in his willingness both to suffer and to concentrate.

Soldiers on active service do not expect a safe or easy time.

They take hardship, risk and suffering as a matter of course. These things are part and parcel of a soldier's calling. As Tertullian put it in his *Address to Martyrs*: 'No soldier comes to the war surrounded by luxuries, nor goes into action from a comfortable bedroom, but from the makeshift and narrow tent, where every kind of hardness and severity and unpleasantness is to be found.'[1] Similarly, the Christian should not expect an easy time. If he is loyal to the gospel, he is sure to experience opposition and ridicule. He must 'share in suffering' with his comrades-in-arms.

The soldier must be willing to concentrate as well as to suffer. When on active service he does not 'get himself entangled in business' (JBP). On the contrary, he frees himself from civilian affairs, in order to give himself to soldiering and so satisfy his superior officers or 'be wholly at his commanding officer's disposal' (JBP). As E. K. Simpson expresses it, 'the spectacle of military discipline furnished a grand lesson of wholeheartedness'.[2] So in the Second World War people frequently said to each other with a wry smile 'there's a war on'—a watchword sufficient to justify any austerity, self-denial or abstention from innocent activities because of the current emergency.

The Christian, who is intended to live in the world and not contract out of it, cannot of course avoid ordinary duties at home, at work and in the community. Indeed as a Christian he should be outstandingly conscientious in doing and not dodging them. Nor should he forget, as Paul reminded Timothy in his first letter, either that 'everything created by God is good, and nothing is to be rejected if it is received with thanksgiving' or that 'God . . . richly furnishes us with everything to enjoy' (1 Tim. 4:4; 6:17). So what is forbidden the good soldier of Jesus Christ is not all 'secular' activities, but rather 'entanglements' which, though they may be perfectly innocent in themselves, may hinder him from fighting Christ's battles. This counsel applies specially to the Christian minister or pastor. He is called to devote himself to teaching and tending Christ's flock, and there are other Scriptures besides this one to say that if

[1] *Address to Martyrs*, chapter 2, para. 3. Alfred Plummer's translation, p. 346.
[2] Simpson, p. 131.

possible he should not have the additional burden of having to get his living in some 'secular' employment.

It is true that the apostle himself had often earned his keep by his tent-making. Yet he made it plain that in his case the reason was personal and exceptional, namely to 'make the gospel free of charge' and so put no possible 'obstacle in the way of the gospel of Christ' (1 Cor. 9:18, 12). He still asserted the principle for himself and for every minister, by command of the Lord, that 'those who proclaim the gospel should get their living by the gospel' (1 Cor. 9:14). Indeed, he clearly expected this to be the general rule. And this needs to be remembered in our day when 'auxiliary', 'supplementary' and 'part-time' ministries are increasing, in which the pastor continues his trade or profession and exercises his ministry in his spare time. Such ministries can hardly be said to contravene Scripture. Yet they are difficult to reconcile with the apostle's injunction to avoid entanglements. In the Church of England service for the ordination of presbyters the Bishop exhorts the candidates in these words: 'Consider how studious ye ought to be in reading and learning the Scriptures . . . and for this selfsame cause how ye ought to forsake and set aside (as much as you may) all worldly cares and studies, . . . give yourselves wholly to this Office, . . . apply yourselves wholly to this one thing, and draw all your cares and studies this way.'

The application of this verse is wider than to pastors, however. Every Christian is in some degree a soldier of Christ, even if he is as timid as Timothy. For, whatever our temperament, we cannot avoid the Christian conflict. And if we are to be good soldiers of Jesus Christ, we must be dedicated to the battle, committing ourselves to a life of discipline and suffering, and avoiding whatever may 'entangle' us and so distract us from it.

3. METAPHOR II: THE LAW-ABIDING ATHLETE (verse 5)
An athlete is not crowned unless he competes according to the rules.

Paul now turns from the image of the Roman soldier to that of the competitor in the Greek games. In no athletic contest of the ancient world (any more than of the modern) was a competitor giving a random display of strength or skill. Every sport had its

rules, always for the contest itself and sometimes for the prepara-
tory training as well. Every event had its prize also, and the
prizes awarded at the Greek games were evergreen wreaths, not
gold medals or silver trophies. But no athlete, however brilliant,
was 'crowned' unless he had competed 'according to the rules'.
'No rules, no wreath' was the order of the day.

The Christian life is regularly likened in the New Testament
to a race, not in the sense that we are competing against each
other (though we are to 'outdo one another in showing honour',
Rom. 12:10), but in other ways, in the strenuous self-discipline
of training (1 Cor. 9:24–27), in laying aside every hindrance
(Heb. 12:1, 2) and here in keeping the rules.

We are to run the Christian race *nomimōs*, 'lawfully'. In spite of
the strange teaching of the so-called 'new morality', which insists
that the category of law has been abolished by Christ, the
Christian is under obligation to live 'lawfully', to keep the rules,
to obey God's moral laws. True, he is not 'under law' as a way
of salvation, to commend him to God, but he is as a guide to
conduct. So far from abolishing his law God first sent his Son
to die for us 'in order that the just requirement of the law might
be fulfilled in us', and now sends his Spirit to live in us and to
write his law in our hearts! (Rom. 8:3, 4; Je. 31:33). Further,
there is no crown otherwise, not of course because our law-
abiding could ever justify us, but rather because without it we
give evidence that we have never been justified.

The context requires that competing 'according to the rules'
has a wider application than to our moral conduct, however.
Paul is describing Christian service, not just Christian life. He
seems to be saying that rewards for service depend on faithfulness. The Christian teacher must teach the truth, building with
solid materials on the foundation of Christ, if his work is to
endure and not be burned up (*cf.* 1 Cor. 3:10–15). So Timothy
must faithfully pass on the deposit to faithful men. Only if, like
Paul, he perseveres to the end, so that he too fights the good
fight, finishes the race and keeps the faith, can he expect on the
last day to receive that most coveted of all wreaths, 'the crown
of righteousness' (2 Tim. 4:7, 8).

4. METAPHOR III: THE HARDWORKING FARMER
(verse 6)

It is the hardworking farmer who ought to have the first share of the crops.

If the athlete must play fair, the farmer must work hard. He 'toils' at his job, as the verb indicates. Hard work is indeed indispensable to good farming. This is particularly so in developing countries before mechanization arrives. In such circumstances successful farming depends as much on sweat as on skill. However poor the soil, inclement the weather, or disinclined the farmer, he must keep at his work. Having put his hand to the plough, he must not look back. Bishop Moule writes of 'the strenuous and prosaic toil' of the farmer. Unlike the soldier and the athlete the farmer's life is 'totally devoid of excitement, remote from all glamour of peril and of applause'.[1]

Yet the first share of the crops goes to the hardworking farmer. He deserves it. His good yield is due as much to his toil and perseverance as to anything else. That is why a sluggard never makes a good farmer, as the book of Proverbs insists. He always loses his harvest, either because he is asleep when he ought to be reaping, or because he was too lazy to plough the previous autumn, or because he has allowed his fields to become overgrown with nettles and thorns (Pr. 10:5; 20:4; 24:30, 31).

To what kind of harvest is the apostle referring? Two applications are more obviously biblical than others.

First, holiness is a harvest. True, it is 'the fruit (or 'harvest') of the Spirit', in that the Spirit is himself the chief farmer who produces a good crop of Christian qualities in the believer's life. But we have our part to play. We are to 'walk by the Spirit' and 'sow to the Spirit' (Gal. 5:16; 6:8), following his promptings and disciplining ourselves, if we would reap the harvest of holiness. Many Christians are surprised that they are not noticeably growing in holiness. Is it that we are neglecting to cultivate the field of our character? 'Whatever a man sows, that he will also reap' (Gal. 6:7). As Bishop Ryle emphasizes again and again in

[1] Moule, p. 77.

his great book entitled *Holiness*, there are 'no gains without pains'. For example:

> 'I will never shrink from declaring my belief that there are no "spiritual gains without pains". I should as soon expect a farmer to prosper in business who contented himself with sowing his fields and never looking at them till harvest, as expect a believer to attain much holiness who was not diligent about his Bible-reading, his prayers, and the use of his Sundays. Our God is a God who works by means, and He will never bless the soul of that man who pretends to be so high and spiritual that he can get on without them.'[1]

As Paul puts it here, it is 'the hardworking farmer' who has the first share of the crop. For holiness is a harvest.

Secondly, the winning of converts is a harvest too. 'The harvest is plentiful,' Jesus said, referring to the many who are waiting to hear and receive the gospel (Mt. 9:37; *cf.* Jn. 4:35; Rom. 1:13). Now in this harvest it is of course 'God who gives the growth' (1 Cor. 3:6, 7). But again we have no liberty to be idle. Further, both the sowing of the good seed of God's word and the reaping of the harvest are hard work, especially when the labourers are few. Souls are hardly won for Christ, not by the slick, automatic application of a formula, but by tears and sweat and pain, especially in prayer and in sacrificial personal friendship. Again, it is 'the hardworking farmer' who can expect good results.

This notion that Christian service is hard work is so unpopular in some happy-go-lucky Christian circles today that I feel the need to underline it. I have already mentioned that the verb signifies to 'toil'. Arndt and Gingrich say that it means first of all to 'become weary, tired' and so to 'work hard, toil, strive, struggle'. Both the noun (*kopos*) and the verb (*kopiaō*) were favourite words with Paul, and it may be healthy for us to see what strong exertion he believed to be necessary in Christian service.

It goes without saying that the word can be used of manual labour, and Paul applied it to his tent-making. 'We labour,' he could write, 'working with our own hands' (1 Cor. 4:12; *cf.*

---

[1] *Holiness* by J. C. Ryle (James Clarke, 1952), p. 21.

Eph. 4:28; 1 Thes. 4:11). But in his view spiritual work involved exertion too. He was quick to recognize thoroughness
in others and sent special greetings at the end of his Roman letter
to 'Mary who has worked hard among you' and to 'the beloved
Persis who has worked hard in the Lord' (Rom. 16:6, 12b). Not
that Paul expected more of others than he was prepared to give
himself. His exertions for the gospel were phenomenal. He could
write of 'labours, watching, hunger' because, like his Master
before him, he was often too busy to sleep or to eat, and could
claim in respect of the other apostles, 'I worked harder than any
of them' (2 Cor. 6:5; 1 Cor. 15:10; cf. Gal. 4:11; Phil. 2:16).
If we were to press him about the nature of this toil, I think he
would reply in terms of those two apostolic priorities 'prayer
and . . . the ministry of the word' (Acts 6:4). For he alluded in
his first letter to Timothy to those elders 'who labour in preaching and teaching' (1 Tim. 5:17), and described to the Colossians
his 'toil, striving with all the energy which he mightily inspires
within me' (Col. 1:29–2:1; cf. 1 Tim. 4:10) in a context which
seems to refer to the prayer-battle in which he was engaged on
their behalf.

The blessing of God rested upon the ministry of the apostle
Paul in quite exceptional measure. No doubt many explanations
of this could be given. But I find myself wondering if we attribute it sufficiently to the zeal and zest, the almost obsessional
devotion, with which he gave himself to the work. He gave and
did not count the cost; he fought and did not heed the wounds;
he toiled and did not seek for rest; he laboured and asked for no
reward except the joy of doing his Lord's will. And God pros-
pered his efforts. Again, it is 'the hardworking farmer' who gets
a good crop.

So far, then, we have looked at the first three metaphors with
which Paul illustrates the duties of the Christian worker. By
them he has isolated three aspects of wholeheartedness which
should be found in Timothy, and in all those who like Timothy
seek to pass on to others 'the good deposit' they have themselves
received: the dedication of a good soldier, the law-abiding
obedience of a good athlete and the painstaking labour of a good
farmer. Without these we cannot expect results. There will be
no victory for the soldier unless he gives himself to his soldiering,

no wreath for the athlete unless he keeps the rules, and no
harvest for the farmer unless he toils at his farming.

5. THE WAY TO UNDERSTANDING (verse 7)

*Think over what I say, for the Lord will grant you understanding in
everything.*

This verse concludes the first paragraph of the chapter. There is
an important biblical balance here. If Timothy is to know and
understand the truth, not least as expressed in the metaphors
Paul has just employed, two processes will be necessary, the one
human and the other divine. Timothy himself must 'think over'
or 'reflect on' (NEB) the apostle's teaching, listening to it carefully
and applying his mind to it. For then the Lord will grant him
understanding in everything. According to this better text, which
the RSV follows, what Paul here expresses is a promise, and not
merely a wish.

There are at least two important implications of this combination of human study and divine illumination for anybody who
wants to inherit the promised gift of understanding from the
Lord.

First, if we are to receive understanding from the Lord, we
must consider what *the apostle* is saying. This is a good example
of Paul's self-conscious apostolic authority. He commands
Timothy to ponder his teaching and promises that the Lord
will grant him 'understanding in everything' if he does so. He
sees nothing anomalous about claiming that his teaching as an
apostle merits careful study, or that it can be interpreted by the
Lord alone, or that this is the way for Timothy to grow in
understanding. It is clear evidence that Paul believed his teaching
to be not his own but the Lord's. Indeed, in the following verses,
almost imperceptibly, he equates 'my gospel' (8) with 'the word
of God' (9).

Secondly, if we are to receive understanding from the Lord,
we must *consider* what the apostle is saying. Some Christians never
get down to any serious Bible study. The reason may of course
be purely 'carnal', namely that they are too lazy. Alternatively,
it may be 'spiritual' (though I fear I would have to call it 'pseudo-

spiritual'), namely that they believe understanding will come to them from the Holy Spirit and not from their own studies (which is a totally false antithesis). So all they do is to skim through some Bible verses in a haphazard and desultory fashion, hoping (and even praying) that the Holy Spirit will show them what it all means. But they do not obey the apostle's command, 'Think over what I say.'

Others are very good at Bible study. They are 'hardworking farmers', as it were. They use their minds and grapple with the text of Scripture. They compare versions, consult concordances and pore over commentaries. But they forget that it is the Lord alone who imparts understanding, and that he imparts it as a gift.

So we must not divorce what God has joined together. For the understanding of Scripture a balanced combination of thought and prayer is essential. We must do the considering, and the Lord will do the giving of understanding.

6. SUFFERING A CONDITION OF BLESSING (verses 8–13)

*Remember Jesus Christ, risen from the dead, descended from David, as preached in my gospel, *[9]*the gospel for which I am suffering and wearing fetters like a criminal. But the word of God is not fettered.* [10]*Therefore I endure everything for the sake of the elect, that they also may obtain the salvation in Christ Jesus with its eternal glory.* [11]*The saying is sure:*

If we have died with him, we shall also live with him;
[12]*if we endure, we shall also reign with him;*
if we deny him, he also will deny us;
[13]*if we are faithless, he remains faithful—*
for he cannot deny himself.

We come now to a new paragraph before the apostle introduces three more metaphors to illustrate the role of the Christian worker. So far we may summarize his theme by the epigram 'nothing that is easy is ever worth while', or rather the reverse 'nothing that is worth while is ever easy'. No soldier, athlete or farmer expects results without labour or suffering. Here Paul continues the same theme. But having illustrated it by metaphor, he goes on to enforce it from experience—the experience first of Christ (8), then of himself as an apostle (9, 10) and lastly of all Christian believers (11–13).

a. The experience of Christ (verse 8)

The command to 'remember Jesus Christ' at first sight seems extraordinary. How could Timothy ever forget him? Yet the human memory is notoriously fickle: it is possible to forget even one's own name! The epitaph over Israel's grave was 'they soon forgot', and it was to overcome our forgetfulness of Christ crucified that he deliberately instituted his supper as a feast of remembrance, a fragrant 'forget-me-not'. Even so the church has often forgotten Jesus Christ, absorbing itself instead now in barren theological debate, now in purely humanitarian activity, now in its own petty, parochial business.

How and why, then, are we to remember Christ? Essentially because he is the gospel, the heart of the good deposit. Indeed, Paul expresses it, he is the heart of 'my gospel', the gospel 'not invented by me but entrusted to me',[1] like 'my deposit' (1:12). So then, if Timothy is to guard the deposit, and to hand it on faithfully to others, he must 'remember Jesus Christ . . . as preached in my gospel'.

In particular, Christ is to be remembered as the one who is both 'risen from the dead' and 'descended from David'. As we meditate on these two expressions, it is remarkable how full an account of the gospel they give. The birth, death, resurrection and ascension of Jesus are all implicit in them. And these remind us both of his divine-human person and of his saving work.

First, his person. The words 'descended from David' imply his humanity, for they speak of his earthly descent from David. The words 'risen from the dead' imply his divinity, for he was powerfully designated God's Son by his resurrection from the dead.[2]

Secondly, his work. The phrase 'risen from the dead' indicates that he died for our sins and was raised to prove the efficacy of

---

[1] Lock, p. 95.
[2] Rom. 1:4. Note that in Rom. 1:3 Jesus is also described as 'descended from David according to the flesh'.

his sinbearing sacrifice. The phrase 'descended from David' indicates that he has established his kingdom as great David's greater Son (*cf.* Lk. 1:32, 33). Taken together, the two phrases seem to allude to his double role as Saviour and King.

There is another reason why Timothy must 'remember Jesus Christ, risen from the dead, descended from David'. It is not just because these facts constitute the gospel which Timothy must preach, but because they also illustrate, from Jesus Christ's own experience, the principle that death is the gateway to life and suffering the path to glory. For he who died rose from the dead, and he who was born in lowliness as David's seed is now reigning in glory on David's throne. Both expressions set forth in embryonic form the contrast between humiliation and exaltation.

'So then, Timothy,' the apostle seems to be saying, 'when you are tempted to avoid pain, humiliation, suffering or death in your ministry, remember Jesus Christ and think again!'

b. The experience of the apostle Paul (verses 9, 10)

Paul is suffering for the gospel. He is having to endure the painful indignity of wearing chains 'like a common criminal' (NEB)—the only other occurrence of the word in the New Testament is of the criminals crucified with Jesus (Lk. 23:32, 33) —although he is a Roman citizen and an innocent man. But, though he is chained, God's word is not. Even he himself at his first defence had been given the opportunity and the strength fully to proclaim God's word to the court, as he will later explain to Timothy in greater detail (4:16, 17). In addition, God's word could spread (was spreading) through many others, and in particular Timothy must share increasingly in this work.

The relation between Paul's sufferings and the effectiveness of the gospel is not just one of contrast, however: 'I am chained; God's word is not.' It is actually one of cause and effect: 'Therefore I endure everything for the sake of the elect, that they also may obtain . . . salvation.' We notice in passing that the doctrine of election does not dispense with the necessity of preaching. On the contrary, it makes it essential. For Paul preaches and suffers for it (literally) 'in order that' they 'may obtain the salvation in Christ Jesus with its eternal glory'. The elect obtain

salvation in Christ not apart from the preaching of Christ but
by means of it.

Further, it is not just the preaching but also the resultant
suffering which are the means of the elect's salvation. Paul's
statement that in some sense the salvation of others is secured by
his sufferings may at first astonish us. Yet it is so. Not of course
that his sufferings have any redemptive efficacy like Christ's, but
that the elect are saved through the gospel and that he could not
preach the gospel without suffering for it. It is another case of
'glory through suffering', the 'eternal glory' of the elect through
the sufferings endured by the apostle.

c. Our common Christian experience (verses 11-13)

Paul now quotes a current saying or fragment of an early
Christian hymn which he pronounces reliable.[1] It consists of two
pairs of epigrams, which are general axioms of Christian life and
experience. They apply equally to all believers. The first pair
relates to those who remain true and endure, the second pair to
those who become false and faithless.

> 'If we have died with him, we shall also live with him;
> if we endure, we shall also reign with him' (11b, 12a).

The death with Christ which is here mentioned must refer,
according to the context, not to our death to *sin* through union
with Christ in his death, but rather to our death to *self* and to
safety, as we take up the cross and follow Christ. The former
Paul describes in Romans 6:3 ('do you not know that all of us
who have been baptized into Christ Jesus were baptized into his
death?'); the latter he expresses both in 1 Corinthians 15:31 ('I
die every day') and in 2 Corinthians 4:10 ('always carrying in
the body the death of Jesus'). That this is the meaning in the
hymn fragments seems plain from the fact that to 'have died with
Christ' and to 'endure' are parallel expressions.

So the Christian life is depicted as a life of dying, a life of
enduring. Only if we share Christ's death on earth, shall we share

---

[1] There are four similar quotations in the Pastorals introduced by
the formula 'the saying is sure', namely in 1 Tim. 1:15; 3:1; 4:9 and
Tit. 3:8.

his life in heaven. Only if we share his sufferings and endure, shall we share his reign in the hereafter. For the road to life is death, and the road to glory suffering (*cf.* Rom. 8:17; 2 Cor. 4:17).

> 'If we deny him, he also will deny us;
> if we are faithless, he remains faithful—for he cannot deny himself' (12b, 13).

This other pair of epigrams envisages the dreadful possibility of our denying Christ and proving faithless. The first phrase 'if we deny him, he also will deny us' seems to be an echo of our Lord's own warning: 'whoever denies me before men, I also will deny before my Father who is in heaven' (Mt. 10:33).

What then of the second phrase 'if we are faithless, he remains faithful'? It has often been taken as a comforting assurance that, even if we turn away from Christ, he will not turn away from us, for he will never be faithless as we are. And it is true, of course, that God never exhibits the fickleness or the faithlessness of man. Yet the logic of the Christian hymn, with its two pairs of balancing epigrams, really demands a different interpretation. 'If we deny him' and 'if we are faithless' are parallels, which requires that 'he will deny us' and 'he remains faithful' be parallels also. In this case his 'faithfulness' when we are faithless will be faithfulness to his warnings. As William Hendriksen puts it: 'Faithfulness on his part means carrying out his threats . . . as well as his promises.'[1] So he will deny us, as the earlier epigram asserts. Indeed, if he did not deny us (in faithfulness to his plain warnings), he would then deny himself. But one thing is certain about God beyond any doubt or uncertainty whatever, and that is 'he cannot deny himself'.

The idea that there may be something which God 'cannot' do is entirely foreign to some people. Can he not do anything and everything? Are not all things possible to him? Is he not omnipotent? Yes, but God's omnipotence needs to be understood. God is not a totalitarian tyrant that he should exercise his power arbitrarily and do absolutely anything whatsoever. God's omnipotence is the freedom and the power to do absolutely anything he chooses to do. But he chooses only to do good, only to

[1] Hendriksen, p. 260.

work according to the perfection of his character and will. God can do everything consistent with being himself. The one and only thing he cannot do, because he will not, is to deny himself or act contrary to himself. So God remains for ever himself, the same God of mercy and of justice, fulfilling his promises (whether of blessing or of judgment), giving us life if we die with Christ and a kingdom if we endure, but denying us if we deny him, just as he warned, because he cannot deny himself.

Looking back over the first half of this chapter (verses 1 to 13), the apostle Paul seems to have been hammering home a single lesson. From secular analogy (soldiers, athletes, farmers) and from spiritual experience (Christ's, his own, every Christian's) he has been insisting that blessing comes through pain, fruit through toil, life through death, and glory through suffering. It is an invariable law of Christian life and service.

So why should we expect things to be easy for us or promise an easy time to others? Neither human wisdom nor divine revelation gives us such an expectation. Why then do we deceive ourselves and others? The truth is the reverse, namely 'no pains, no gains' or 'no cross, no crown'.

It is this principle which took Jesus Christ through a lowly birth and a shameful death to his glorious resurrection and heavenly reign. It is this principle which had brought Paul his chains and prison cell, in order that the elect might obtain salvation and glory. It is the same principle which makes the soldier willing to endure hardship, the athlete discipline and the farmer toil. It would be ridiculous, therefore, to expect our Christian life and service to cost us nothing.

In the second part of 2 Timothy 2 (verses 14–26), Paul continues his vivid portrayal of Timothy in his role of teaching and transmitting the faith, and therefore by derivation of every Christian minister, teacher or worker. He now uses three more metaphors—the 'workman who has no need to be ashamed' (15), the 'vessel for noble use' (21) and 'the Lord's servant' (24). Each adds a further feature to the portrait.

7. METAPHOR IV: THE UNASHAMED WORKMAN
(verses 14–19)

Remind them of this, and charge them before the Lord to avoid disputing about words, which does no good, but only ruins the hearers. [15] *Do your best to present yourself to God as one approved, a workman who has no need to be ashamed, rightly handling the word of truth.* [16] *Avoid such godless chatter, for it will lead people into more and more ungodliness,* [17] *and their talk will eat its way like gangrene. Among them are Hymenaeus and Philetus,* [18] *who have swerved from the truth by holding that the resurrection is past already. They are upsetting the faith of some.* [19] *But God's firm foundation stands, bearing this seal: 'The Lord knows those who are his,' and, 'Let every one who names the name of the Lord depart from iniquity.'*

We will leave verse 14 aside for the moment and proceed straight to verse 15. Several facts are immediately evident from this exhortation to Timothy to aim to be an unashamed workman.

First, the kind of work the Christian workman does is teaching. He is called to handle 'the word of truth'.

Secondly, there are two kinds of workman. On the one hand, there are those who are 'approved', 'tried and true' (AG), who having been tested like coins or metals and passed the test are recognized as 'sterling';[1] on the other hand there are those who are not approved, because they fail the test. The former group have 'no need to be ashamed', while the latter ought to be deeply ashamed of themselves.

Thirdly, the difference between these two categories concerns their handling or treatment of 'the word of truth', the good deposit.

So Paul sets these two kinds of teacher in contrast, and supplies an example of each. Timothy (15) is to be a good workman, approved and not ashamed. Hymenaeus and Philetus (17), however, are bad workmen who have forfeited God's approval (whatever approval they may have obtained from men) and have every reason to be ashamed.

Further, the work of these good and bad workmen is summed

[1] Simpson, p. 136.

up in pregnant verbs. The good workman 'cuts straight' (15, literally) the word of truth; the bad workman 'swerves' (18) or deviates from the truth. We must look at these more fully and separately.

a. The good workman

The verb in verse 15 (*orthotomeō*), translated in RSV 'rightly handling' means literally not to 'divide rightly' (AV) but to 'cut straight'. It is a very unusual word and occurs three times only in biblical Greek, once in the New Testament (this verse) and twice in the book of Proverbs, where in 3:6 we read 'He will make straight your paths', and in 11:5 'The righteousness of the blameless keeps his way straight'.

How then is 'the word of truth' being pictured that Timothy is commanded to make or cut it straight? Not as a sacrificial victim to be cut into pieces, as some ancient commentators thought; nor as a loaf, so that 'Paul assigns to teachers the duty of carving or dividing the Word, like a father dividing the bread into small pieces to feed the children';[1] nor as a ribbon to be cut into strips, or a plot into allotments, as some modern dispensationalists teach; nor even, I think, as a stone which masons cut to fit into a building, as C. K. Barrett suggests;[2] but rather as a road or path or—to be more modern—as a motorway or freeway needs to be cut straight through the countryside. Thus, Arndt and Gingrich define the verb as meaning to ' "cut a path in a straight direction" or "cut a road across country (that is forested or otherwise difficult to pass through) in a straight direction", so that the traveller may go directly to his destination'. Or, possibly, the metaphor may be taken rather from ploughing than from roadmaking, so that the NEB, following Chrysostom, renders it 'driving a straight furrow in your proclamation of the truth'.

'The word of truth' is the apostolic faith which Timothy has received from Paul and is to communicate to others. For us it is, quite simply, Scripture. To 'cut it straight' or 'make it a straight path' is to be accurate on the one hand and plain on the other in our exposition. Apparently Sophocles used the word for 'to expound soundly' (MM). Thus the good workman is true to

---

[1] Calvin, p. 313. [2] Barrett, p. 105.

Scripture. He does not falsify it.[1] Nor does he try to confuse people, like Elymas the sorcerer, by 'making crooked the straight paths of the Lord' (Acts 13:10). On the contrary, he handles the word with such scrupulous care that he both stays on the path himself, keeping to the highway and avoiding the byways, and makes it easy for others to follow.

b. The bad workman

The metaphor Paul employs to describe the bad workman is taken neither from civil engineeering nor from agriculture but from archery. So now the truth is likened not to a road being built or a furrow being ploughed but to a target being shot at. The verb (18) is *astocheō*, which comes from *stochos*, a 'target', and means to 'miss the mark' and so to 'deviate' from something. It occurs three times in the Pastoral Epistles:

> 'Certain persons by swerving from these (*sc.* genuine love, a good conscience and sincere faith) have wandered away into vain discussion' (1 Tim. 1:16). 'For by professing it (*sc.* 'what is falsely called knowledge') some have missed the mark as regards the faith' (1 Tim. 6:21). 'Who have swerved from the truth . . .' or as in NEB, 'shot wide of the truth' (2 Tim. 2:18).

We are now in a position to grasp the alternative which Paul sets before every Christian teacher entrusted with the word of truth, and which determines whether he will be a good or a bad workman.

The word of truth is a target. As he shoots at this target, he will either hit it or miss it.

The word of truth is a road. As he cuts this road through the forest, he will make it either straight or crooked.

As a result of what he does, that is, how he teaches, others are bound to be affected, for better or for worse. If he cuts the road straight, people will be able to follow and so keep in the way. If, on the other hand, he misses the mark, the attention of the

---

[1] *Cf.* 2 Cor. 2:17. It is significant that the noun *orthotomia* was used by both Clement of Alexandria and Eusebius for 'orthodoxy'.

spectators will be distracted from the target and their eyes will follow the arrow however widely astray it has gone.

Of this grave danger Paul warns Timothy here. There were some in Asia who were teaching serious error. Instead of preaching Paul's gospel which included 'Jesus Christ risen from the dead' (8), the pledge and pattern of his people's resurrection, they were saying 'that the resurrection is past already' (18). Of course in one sense it is, in that Christ has risen and his people have already risen with him. Yet the resurrection of the body lies still in the future. The false teachers, however, were denying any bodily resurrection to come (*cf.* Acts 17:32; 1 Cor. 15:12). They were perhaps early Gnostics to whom the body was an evil encumbrance and the concept of any bodily resurrection therefore as inconceivable as it was undesirable. So they 'spiritualized' it as a release from the flesh through *gnōsis* (knowledge), or by asserting that the promise of resurrection had been entirely fulfilled when by faith and baptism we were raised with Christ. Similarly today some 'demythologize' the resurrection and speak only of faith rising in the Christian's heart.

Such heretics were substituting for 'the word of truth' what Paul calls 'disputing about words' (14). The verb he employs here (*logomacheō*) occurs nowhere else in the New Testament, although the noun *logomachia*, 'word-battle' (AG), is found in 1 Timothy 6:4 and some MSS of Titus 3:9. He seems to be referring to something 'like the hair-splittings of the schoolmen'[1] in the middle ages. Elsewhere he calls it 'godless chatter' (16, *kenophōnia* or 'empty talk').[2]

Paul's instruction to Timothy about such bad workmen or false teachers is to 'avoid' them: '. . . charge them before the Lord to avoid disputing about words, which does no good, but only ruins the hearers' (14). 'Avoid such godless chatter, for it will lead people into more and more ungodliness, and their talk will eat its way like gangrene' (16, 17a).

The damage caused by such false teaching is double. It is both 'godless' and 'gangrenous'. That is, in the first place, it leads people away from God. What verse 16 literally says is that those who hold such teaching 'advance into more and more ungodli-

[1] Simpson, p. 136.
[2] The only other occurrence of this word is in 1 Tim. 6:20.

ness'. It is hardly an 'advance', however. As Patrick Fairbairn comments,[1] it is 'a forward movement in the wrong direction'. In the second place, it spreads its infection in the community. Three times Paul reiterates this for emphasis: It 'does no good, but only ruins the hearers' (14b). 'Their teachings are as dangerous as blood poisoning to the body and spread like sepsis from a wound' (17 JBP). 'They are upsetting the faith of some' (18b).

These two tendencies of heresy are most revealing. We would be wise to ask ourselves regarding every kind of teaching both what its attitude is towards God and what effect it has upon men. There is invariably something about error which is dishonouring to God and damaging to men. The truth, on the other hand, always honours God, promoting godliness (cf. Tit. 1:16), and always edifies its hearers. Instead of causing a katastrophē (14), upsetting them or turning them upside down, it builds them up in faith, love and holiness.

Although the faith of men can be upset (18b), the foundation of God remains secure. This is the true church which he is building. It has a twofold 'seal' or 'inscription' (JBP, NEB). The first is secret and invisible, namely 'The Lord knows those who are his' and will therefore keep them safe for ever. The second is public and visible, namely 'Let everyone who names the name of the Lord depart from iniquity', and so let him prove that he belongs to the Lord by his holiness. The reference is probably to the Old Testament story of the rebellion of Korah, Dathan and Abiram, from which incident both quotations come (Nu. 16:5, 26). Ultimately, Paul is saying, it is only the Lord who knows and recognizes his own people, and can tell the true from the spurious, for only he sees the heart. But though we cannot see the heart, we can see the life, which is the one reliable evidence of the heart's condition, and is apparent to all. Both 'seals' are essential, however, the divine and the human, the unseen and the seen. Together they bear witness to 'God's firm foundation', his true church.

It is doubtless the reference to the necessity of departing from evil which leads Paul to the next metaphor.

[1] Fairbairn, p. 345.

8. METAPHOR V: THE CLEAN VESSEL (verses 20-22)

In a great house there are not only vessels of gold and silver but also of wood and earthenware, and some for noble use, some for ignoble. [21]*If any one purifies himself from what is ignoble, then he will be a vessel for noble use, consecrated and useful to the master of the house, ready for any good work.* [22] *So shun youthful passions and aim at righteousness, faith, love, and peace, along with those who call upon the Lord from a pure heart.*

The picture which the apostle is conjuring up is clear. Every house is equipped with vessels or utensils of different kinds, pots and pans and dishes and the like. In a 'great house' or stately mansion these are many and varied. They may be divided approximately into two groups. There are the 'vessels of gold and silver', which are 'for noble use', possibly 'for special occasions' (JB), and in particular for the personal service of the master of the house. There are also vessels 'of wood and earthenware', which, apart from being of cheaper quality in themselves, are reserved for *ignoble* or menial use in the kitchen and the scullery.

To what is the apostle alluding by this metaphor? There can be little doubt that the 'great house' is God's house, the visible or professing church. But what are the 'vessels'? The use of the term elsewhere in the New Testament suggests that they stand not simply for members of the church, but for the church's teachers. For example, Jesus had said to Ananias about the newly converted Saul of Tarsus: 'he is a chosen instrument of mine to carry my name before the Gentiles and kings and the sons of Israel' (Acts 9:15). Years later Paul described himself and his fellow-workers by a similar image when he wrote: 'we have this treasure in earthen vessels' (2 Cor. 4:7). In these verses 'instrument' and 'vessel' translate the same Greek word (*skeuos*) as Paul is now using in his letter to Timothy. A *skeuos* was any kind of utensil. It is true that when he called himself an *earthen* vessel he was applying the metaphor differently, for he was there emphasizing his physical infirmity, and not implying that he was fit only for ignoble use. Nevertheless, the theme of service is prominent in each verse. As a 'vessel' Paul's function was to carry Christ's name before unbelievers, and in the earthenware vessel he carried the treasure of the gospel, as a fragile pottery lamp carries the light.

From this usage I think we would be justified in concluding that the two sets of vessels in the great house (gold and silver for noble use, wood and earthenware for ignoble) represent not genuine and spurious members of the church but true and false teachers in the church. Paul is still, in fact, referring to the two sets of teachers he has contrasted in the previous paragraph, the authentic like Timothy and the bogus like Hymenaeus and Alexander. The only difference is that he changes the metaphor from good and bad workmen to noble and ignoble vessels.

It would be difficult to exaggerate the privilege which the apostle here sets before Timothy in verse 21. Indeed he extends it to any and every Christian minister or worker who will fulfil the condition, for his statement is couched in quite general terms: 'if anyone purifies himself'. The privilege is described by simple, yet beautiful expressions. 'He will be a vessel for noble use.' This is then elaborated by three further expressions: 'consecrated' (permanently set apart), 'useful (or 'serviceable') to the master of the house' and 'ready for any good work'. No higher honour could be imagined than to be an instrument in the hand of Jesus Christ, to be at his disposal for the furtherance of his purposes, to be available whenever wanted for his service.

The master of the house lays down only one condition. The vessels which he uses must be clean. His promise hinges on this. It is evident at once that some kind of self-purification is the indispensable condition of usefulness to Christ, but exactly what is it? The words 'from what is ignoble' are the RSV interpretation of *apo toutōn* 'from these' (plural), and 'these' must refer back to the 'vessels for ignoble use' of the previous verse. In what sense, then, are we to purify ourselves from these? It cannot mean that we are to cut adrift from all nominal church members whom we suspect of being spurious, and secede from the visible church, for Jesus indicated in his parable that the weeds had been sown among the wheat and could not be successfully separated from them until the harvest. Besides, we have already seen that it is teachers rather than members who are indicated by the two sorts of vessels. This fact and the context suggest, therefore, that we are to hold ourselves aloof from the kind of false teachers who, like Hymenaeus and Philetus, both deny some fundamental of the gospel and (according to 1 Tim. 1:19, 20) have also violated their conscience and lapsed into some form of unrighteousness. But Paul's condition is more radical even than this. What we are to avoid is not so much contact with such men as their error and their evil. To purify ourselves 'from these' is essentially to purge their falsehood from our minds and their wickedness from our hearts and lives. Purity, then—purity of doctrine and purity of life—is the essential condition of being serviceable to Christ.

That this is the correct interpretation is confirmed by the fact that the metaphor of the great house and its vessels (verses 20 and 21) is sandwiched in between two clear allusions to personal holiness: 'Let every one who names the name of the Lord depart from iniquity' (19) and 'So shun youthful passions and aim at righteousness . . .' (22). It is perfectly true that in his sovereign providence God has sometimes chosen to use impure vessels as the instruments both of his judgment and of his salvation. In Old Testament days he described pagan Assyria as 'the rod of my anger', with which he smote recalcitrant Israel, and which he then discarded (Is. 10:5 ff.). He also called the Babylonian king Nebuchadnezzar 'my servant' through whom he judged his people, and the Persian king Cyrus his 'shepherd' and his 'anointed' through whom he redeemed them (Je. 25:9; 27:6; 43:10 and Is. 44:28; 45:1). But these were exceptional cases; they were also national, rather than personal. The overwhelming emphasis of Scripture is that God chooses to use clean vessels, 'instruments of righteousness' (Rom 6:13), for the fulfilment of his purposes. Certainly in Paul's exhortation to Timothy he must purify himself if he is to be fit for the Master to use.

The apostle now elaborates what he means in an outspoken appeal which is both negative and positive. Negatively, Timothy is to 'shun youthful passions'. This is not to be understood exclusively as a reference to sexual lust, but to 'self-assertion as well as self-indulgence',[1] to selfish ambition, headstrong obstinacy, arrogance and indeed all the 'wayward impulses of youth' (NEB). Positively, Timothy is to 'aim at' the four essential

[1] Lock, p. 101.

marks of a Christian—'righteousness, faith, love and peace'—
and he is to pursue these in good company (maybe to compensate
for the company he will have to avoid if he is to 'purify himself
from what is ignoble'), the company of those 'who call upon
the Lord from a pure heart', that is, who share with Timothy
the same hunger for righteousness and who with unalloyed
sincerity cry to God to satisfy their hunger.

As we listen to Paul's moral exhortation, it is important not to
miss the sharp contrast between its negative and positive aspects
and in particular between the two verbs 'shun' and 'aim at'. Both
are strongly suggestive. *Pheugō* ('shun') means literally to 'seek
safety in flight' or 'escape' (AG). It is used literally of flight from
physical danger, as when Moses fled from Pharaoh's wrath and
the holy family from Herod's (Acts 7:29; Mt. 2:13). So too the
hireling flees from the wolf; and the Judean Christians, when in
AD 70 Jerusalem was surrounded by the legions of Rome, were
to flee to the mountains (Jn. 10:12, 13; Lk. 21:21). In just the
same way, when the verb is used figuratively, it denotes flight
from spiritual danger. All sinners are urged to 'flee from the
wrath to come' (Mt. 3:7). All Christians are commanded to flee
from idolatry, from immorality, from the spirit of materialism
and the love of money, and here from youthful passions (1 Cor.
10:14; 6:18; 1 Tim. 6:11). True, we are also told to withstand
the devil, so that he may flee from us (Jas. 4:7). But we are to
recognize sin as something dangerous to the soul. We are not to
come to terms with it, or even negotiate with it. We are not to
linger in its presence like Lot in Sodom (Gn. 19:15, 16). On
the contrary we are to get as far away from it as possible as
quickly as possible. Like Joseph, when Potiphar's wife attempted
to seduce him, we are to take to our heels and run (Gn. 39:12).

The verb *diōkō* ('aim at') is the exact opposite. For if *pheugō*
means to run away from, *diōkō* means to run after, to 'pursue,
chase, in war or hunting' (LS). Its distinctive literal use in the
New Testament (about 30 times) is of persecution. Paul himself
uses it to describe his pre-conversion activities, how he violently
persecuted God's church (Gal. 1:13) and in his raging fury
against the Christians even harried them out of Jewry into
foreign cities (Acts 26:11). Metaphorically, this verb is used to
portray the Christian's pursuit of the will of God. Under the

figure of a chariot-race Paul describes himself as straining forward
with eagerness, and adds 'I press on' and again 'I press on toward
the goal' (Phil. 3:12, 14). In particular, the Christian is urged[1]
to pursue moral righteousness with the same assiduity with
which the Jews pursued legal righteousness (Rom. 9:31). In
other passages this righteousness or 'holiness' (Heb. 12:14) is
broken up into its constituent parts and supplemented with other
virtues. Thus, we are to go in hot pursuit of 'righteousness, faith,
love and peace' (here) or 'righteousness, godliness, faith, love,
steadfastness, gentleness' (1 Tim. 6:11), or simply 'love' (1 Cor.
14:1), and specially that love for strangers called 'hospitality'
(Rom. 12:13) and the 'good' of others which love always seeks
(1 Thes. 5:15), or simply 'peace', that all-inclusive grace, together
with 'what makes for peace and mutual upbuilding' (Heb. 12:14a;
1 Pet. 3:11 quoting Ps. 34:15; Rom. 14:19). In all these verses
the same verb *diōkō* 'pursue' is used.

So, then, putting back together these two parts of Paul's
exhortation which we have studied in separation, we are both
to run away from spiritual danger and to run after spiritual good,
both to flee from the one in order to escape it and to pursue the
other in order to attain it. This double duty of Christians—
negative and positive—is the consistent, reiterated teaching of
Scripture. Thus, we are to deny ourselves and to follow Christ.
We are to put off what belongs to our old life and to put on what
belongs to our new life. We are to put to death our earthly
members and to set our minds on heavenly things. We are to
crucify the flesh and to walk in the Spirit. It is the ruthless
rejection of the one in combination with the relentless pursuit
of the other which Scripture enjoins upon us as the secret of
holiness. Only so can we hope to be fit for the Master's use. If
the promise is to be inherited ('he will be a vessel for noble use'),
the condition must be fulfilled ('if any one purifies himself from
what is ignoble').

9. METAPHOR VI: THE LORD'S SERVANT (verses 23–26)

*Have nothing to do with stupid, senseless controversies; you know that
they breed quarrels.* 24 *And the Lord's servant must not be quarrel-*

[1] Here and in 1 Tim. 6:11.

some but kindly to every one, an apt teacher, forbearing, [25] *correcting his opponents with gentleness. God may perhaps grant that they will repent and come to know the truth,* [26] *and they may escape from the snare of the devil, after being captured by him to do his will.*

The metaphor changes yet again. The vessel in the house becomes a slave in the household. The *skeuos* is transformed into a *doulos*. But before outlining the kind of behaviour fitting to the Lord's servant, Paul sets the context in which he has to live and work. He reverts to the 'wordy debates' of verse 14 and the 'godless chatter' of verse 16.

The word translated 'controversies' (23) (*zētēsis*, a singular noun) is normally used in one of two senses. It means either an 'investigation', like the legal enquiry into charges against Paul which Festus told King Agrippa he was at a loss to know how to make (Acts 25:20), or a 'discussion' like the debate between the apostles and the Judaizers over circumcision (Acts 15:2, 7). If it is used here in the former sense, it will refer to some kind of philosophical investigation and could be translated 'speculation'. But if it is used in the latter sense, the allusion will be to a 'controversy'.

The word occurs three times in the Pastoral Epistles, once in each letter (1 Tim. 6:4; 2 Tim. 2:23; Tit. 3:9), or four times if the slightly stronger word *ekzētēsis* is added (1 Tim. 1:4). This latter word certainly seems to mean a 'useless speculation' (AG). In the context it is the fruit of a preoccupation with 'myths and endless genealogies'. At the end of the same letter, however, the word *zētēseis* (plural) is coupled with *logomachiai*, meaning 'word-battles', both of which are said to 'produce envy, dissension, slander, base suspicions and wrangling' (1 Tim. 6:4, 5a). So there the emphasis is rather upon heated controversy.

Perhaps there is no need to choose between the two meanings. They certainly appear to be combined in Titus 3:9 where Titus is told to avoid four things—'controversies (*zētēseis*), genealogies (the speculative idea again), dissensions (*ereis*) and quarrels (*machas*, 'battles') over the law'. This last word is prominent in 2 Timothy 2 also, for in verse 23 Paul warns that *zētēseis* 'breed quarrels' (*machas* again), and forbids people, in verse 14, *logomachein* (to dispute about words; *cf.* 1 Tim. 6:4) or in verse 24 *machesthai* (to quarrel or fight). Calvin's expression 'quarrelsome speculation'[1] neatly unites both emphases.

What, then, is being prohibited to Timothy, and through him to all the Lord's servants and ministers today? We cannot conclude that this is a prohibition of all controversy. For when the truth of the gospel was at stake Paul himself had been an ardent controversialist, even to the extent of opposing the apostle Peter to his face in public (Gal. 2:11–14). Besides, in these very Pastoral Epistles he is urging Timothy and Titus to guard the sacred deposit of the truth and contend for it. Every Christian must in some sense 'fight the good fight of the faith' (1 Tim. 6:12; 2 Tim. 4:7), seeking to defend and preserve it. What is forbidden us is controversies which in themselves are 'stupid and senseless' and in their effect 'breed quarrels'. They are 'stupid' or 'futile' (JB) because they are speculative. For the same reason they are 'senseless' (*apaideutos*), literally 'uninstructed' or even 'undisciplined', because they go beyond Scripture and do not submit to the intellectual discipline which Scripture should impose upon us. They also inevitably 'breed quarrels' because when people forsake revelation for speculation, they have no agreed authority and no impartial court of appeal. They lapse into pure subjectivism and so into profitless argument in which one man's opinion is as good (or bad) as another's. If only the church had heeded this warning! The combination of unbiblical speculations and uncharitable polemics has done great damage to the cause of Christ.

The fundamental characteristic of 'the Lord's servant' is to be 'gentleness' (24, 25a). We have already seen that he is called to a teaching ministry. He therefore needs to be 'an apt teacher' (*didaktikos*), endowed with a gift or aptitude for teaching. His instruction will sometimes have to be negative as well as positive. That is to say, he is called not only to teach the truth to the people committed to his care, but also to correct error. He must not shrink from 'correcting his opponents', the 'people who dispute what he says' (JB). But in all his ministry, instructing and correcting alike, he will exhibit the same distinctive quality. He 'must not be quarrelsome'. Instead, he will be 'kindly to everyone . . . forbearing' and characterized by 'gentleness'. The first word

[1] Calvin, p. 312.

(*ēpios*) means 'mild' and is used by Paul to describe the attitude of 'a nurse taking care of her children' (1 Thes. 2:7). The second word (*anexikakos*) means literally 'bearing evil without resentment' (AG) and so forbearing of people's unkindness, patient towards their foolishness and tolerant of their foibles. The last word of the three (*praütēs*) adds to the gentleness portrayed by the other two the notes of 'humility, courtesy, considerateness and meekness' (AG). Its opposite is to be brash, haughty and rude.

All this is the demeanour which is fitting in 'the Lord's servant' and is, of course, deliberately reminiscent of 'the servant of the Lord' portrayed in the 'servant songs' of Isaiah. That servant was a teacher, for the Lord God gave him 'the tongue of those who are taught', and he used it wisely. He knew 'how to sustain with a word him that is weary'. So meek was he in his ministry that he would never shout or make a noise, and so sensitive that he would deal gently with people whose courage had been bruised and whose faith burned low. He would never break a bruised reed or quench a dimly burning wick. And when people rose up in opposition to him he did not resist or retaliate. He gave his back to the smiters, his cheeks to those who pulled out his beard, his face to those who spat upon him, and eventually allowed himself to be led like a sheep silent and unresisting to the slaughter (Is. 50:4; 42:2, 3; 50:6; 53:7). Such was Jesus of Nazareth, the Lord's servant *par excellence*, who described himself as 'gentle and lowly in heart' (Mt. 11:29). And this same 'meekness and gentleness of Christ' (2 Cor. 10:1) must characterize all who claim to be the Lord's servants today.

Moreover, if the Lord's servant adorns his Christian teaching with a Christian character, and if he is meek in his dealings with the wayward, 'correcting his opponents with gentleness', lasting good may follow. God himself, through such a gentle ministry, may perform a conspicuous work of salvation.

We must observe carefully in verses 25b, 26 how these opponents of apostolic truth are regarded. They are evidently sinful, for they need to 'repent', and also in error for they need to 'come to know the truth'. But most striking of all is that the evil and the error in which they are involved are both seen as symptoms of 'the snare of the devil' from whom they need to be rescued. And further, important as is the part played by the gentle servant of the Lord in correcting them, it is God who gives or grants (*dōē*) them repentance, God who illumines their mind to acknowledge the truth, and God who liberates them from Satan's power.

Although the RSV is not incorrect in its rendering of the first two as separate stages ('repent and come to know the truth'), the Greek expression is literally 'grant them repentance unto (*eis*) acknowledgment of truth', thus making their acknowledgment of the truth the consequence of their repentance. It is a good example of the strong link which Scripture everywhere forges between the moral and the intellectual. Everybody knows that our belief conditions our behaviour, but not everybody is so clear that our behaviour also conditions our belief. Just as to violate our conscience leads to the shipwreck of our faith (1 Tim. 1:19), so to repent of our sin leads to an acknowledgment of the truth.

There is some uncertainty about the last phrase of verse 26 'after being captured by him to do his will'. It is not clear whether the *him* (who captures them) and the *his* (whose will they do) relate to God or to the devil. Some commentators think that both refer to God and thus describe the divine capture which secures the people's escape from the devil. They are 'caught now by God and made subject to his will' (NEB mg.). The verb 'captured' is *zōgreō* and means to 'capture alive' (AG). Its only other New Testament use is in Luke 5:10, where Jesus tells Peter the fisherman that in future he will 'catch men'. Perhaps for this reason some commentators attribute the capture to the Lord's servant himself; *e.g.* Lock: 'May it not even be that I shall be a fisher of men, and save them alive, and bring them back to do their true Master's will?'[1]

Others think that the captivity is the devil's, although the will is God's. In this case the people 'escape from the snare of the devil after being captured by him, to do his (that is, God's) will' (RSV mg.).

But most commentators seem to follow AV and RSV in taking both 'him' and 'his' as relating to the devil. In this case the phrase is simply enlarging on what is meant by the snare of Satan. In it 'the devil caught them and kept them enslaved' (JB). If this is correct, it enables us to see behind stage in every

[1] Lock, p. 98.

Christian evangelistic and teaching ministry. Behind the scenes, invisible to men on the stage and in the audience, a spiritual battle is being fought out. The devil's grim activity is graphically depicted. He is likened to a hunter who captures his quarry alive in some clever 'snare' or trap. He also drugs or inebriates them, for the word used of his captives' escape (*ananēphō*) means literally to 'become sober' or 'come to one's senses again' (AG) after a period of diabolical intoxication. From such a captivity, in which men are both trapped and doped by the devil, only God can deliver them by giving them repentance unto an acknowledgment of the truth. Yet he effects the rescue through the human ministry of one of his servants, who avoids quarrelling and teaches with kindness, forbearance and gentleness.

Looking back over the chapter, we are now able to picture in our minds the composite portrait of the ideal Christian minister or worker which Paul has been painting with a variety of words and images. As good soldiers, law-abiding athletes and hardworking farmers, we must be utterly dedicated to our work. As unashamed workmen we must be accurate and clear in our exposition. As vessels for noble use we must be righteous in our character and conduct. And as the Lord's servants we must be courteous and gentle in our manner. Thus each metaphor concentrates on a particular characteristic which contributes to the portrait as a whole, and in fact lays down a condition of usefulness. Only if we give ourselves without reserve to our soldiering, running and farming can we expect results. Only if we cut the truth straight and do not swerve from it shall we be approved by God and have no need to be ashamed. Only if we purify ourselves from what is ignoble, from all sin and error, shall we be vessels for noble use, serviceable to the Master of the house. Only if we are gentle and not quarrelsome, as the Lord's true servants, will God grant our adversaries repentance, knowledge of the truth and deliverance from the devil.

Such is our heavy responsibility to labour and suffer for the gospel. No wonder the chapter began with an exhortation to 'be strong in the grace that is in Christ Jesus'.

Chapter 3

THE CHARGE TO CONTINUE IN THE GOSPEL

AS he lies in his cell, a prisoner of the Lord, Paul is still preoccupied with the future of the gospel. His mind dwells now on the evil of the times, now on the diffidence of Timothy. Timothy is so weak, and the opposition so strong. It seems anomalous that such a man should be called in such a situation to contend for the truth. So the apostle begins with a vivid sketch of the contemporary scene, and against this background summons Timothy—in spite of the almost universal declension from God and in spite of his own temperamental infirmity—to continue faithful to what he has learned.

1. FACING TIMES OF STRESS (verses 1, 2a)

But understand this, that in the last days there will come times of stress.
²For men will be lovers of self . . .

Why does Paul introduce this chapter with such an emphatic command to Timothy to 'understand this'? After all, the existence of active opposition to the gospel was evident. Paul himself had been arrested, chained and imprisoned because of his own loyalty to it (1:11, 12; 2:9). Everybody in Asia had repudiated him, as Timothy was well aware (1:15). And earlier in the letter the apostle has urged his young friend not to be ashamed of the gospel, but to take his share of suffering as Christ's good soldier; has reminded him that he must endure with Christ if he hopes one day to reign with him; and has warned him that behind the 'word-battles', 'godless chatter' and 'stupid and senseless controversies' spread by false teachers there lurks the evil figure of the devil himself (1:8; 2:3, 11–12, 14, 16, 23, 26). So why does the apostle enjoin Timothy to understand what he already knows?

Surely because he wants to emphasize that opposition to the truth is not a passing situation, but a permanent characteristic of the age. Perhaps he fears that Timothy will be over-optimistic, hoping that if he lies low for a while, the storm will pass. But Paul gives him no such hope. We too should 'understand this', and be quite clear about the perils and troubles which will beset us if we stand firm in the truth of the gospel.

Next, Paul refers to 'the last days'. It may seem natural to apply this term to a future epoch, to the days immediately preceding the end when Christ returns. But biblical usage will not allow us to do this. For it is the conviction of the New Testament authors that the new age (promised in the Old Testament) arrived with Jesus Christ, and that therefore with his coming the old age had begun to pass away and the last days had dawned. Thus Peter on the Day of Pentecost quoted Joel's prophecy that 'in the last days' God would pour out his Spirit upon all flesh, and declared that this prophecy had now been fulfilled. 'This is what was spoken by the prophet Joel,' he said. In other words, 'the last days' to which the prophecy referred had come (Acts 2:14-17). Similarly, the Letter to the Hebrews begins with an assertion that the God who had spoken of old to the fathers through the prophets had 'in these last days' spoken to us through his Son (1:1, 2). This being so, we are living in the last days. They were ushered in by Jesus Christ, God's Son.

What follows in 2 Timothy 3, therefore, is a description of the present, not the future. Paul depicts the whole period elapsing between the first and second comings of Christ. 'Under *the last days* he includes the universal condition of the Christian Church.'[1] This not only follows from the way in which the expression 'the last days' is used in the New Testament. It is also plain from the fact that what Paul gives Timothy here is not predictions about some future epoch which he will not himself live to see, but instructions relating to his present ministry, including (for example) the command to 'avoid' certain people (5).[2] Timothy

---

[1] Calvin, p. 322.
[2] Similarly, the backsliders and the scoffers who belong to 'the last days' or the 'later times' and are referred to in 1 Tim. 4:1, 2 Pet. 3:3 and Jude 18 are regarded as already active when Paul, Peter and Jude were writing.

is already living in 'the last days' to which Paul is referring. And so are we. They may get worse in the future (13), but even now the times are bad and perilous.

In these last days, Paul adds, 'there will come times of stress'. What Timothy is to understand about the last days is not that they are uniformly, continuously evil, but that they will include 'perilous seasons' (AV). Church history confirms that this has been so. As the vessel of the Christian church put out to sea, it was not to expect a smooth untroubled passage; it has been buffeted by storms and tempests and even hurricanes.

These seasons Paul denotes as 'times of stress'. The Greek adjective *chalepos* means basically 'hard' or 'difficult', and implies either 'hard to bear' (for example, in the case of physical or mental pain) or 'hard to deal with, violent, dangerous' (AG), 'menacing'.[1] The word was used in classical Greek both of dangerous wild animals and of the raging sea. Its only other New Testament occurrence is in the story of the two Gadarene demoniacs who were as savage and untamed as wild beasts and whom Matthew describes as 'so *fierce* (*chalepos*) that no one could pass that way' (Mt. 8:28). This gives us an idea of the kind of seasons which the church must expect in the last days. They will be both painful and perilous, hard to endure and hard to cope with.

Paul goes on immediately to tell us why this is so: *For men will be* . . . It is important to grasp that it is *men* who are responsible for the menacing seasons which the church has to bear, fallen men, evil men, men whose nature is perverted, whose behaviour is self-centred and godless, whose mind is hostile to God and his law (*cf.* Rom. 8:7), and who spread evil, heresy and dead religion in the church.

Before we study in detail Paul's characterization of these men, we need to absorb his words of introduction. First, we are living in the last days, he says; Christ brought them with him when he came. Secondly, these days will include seasons of peril and stress. Thirdly, they will be the result of the activities of bad men. Fourthly, we are to understand this, to be quite clear about it, and so to be prepared.

[1] Simpson, p. 143.

2. THE EVIL MEN ARE DESCRIBED (verses 2–9)

For men will be lovers of self, lovers of money, proud, arrogant, abusive, disobedient to their parents, ungrateful, unholy, ³inhuman, implacable, slanderers, profligates, fierce, haters of good, ⁴treacherous, reckless, swollen with conceit, lovers of pleasure rather than lovers of God, ⁵holding the form of religion but denying the power of it. Avoid such people. ⁶For among them are those who make their way into households and capture weak women, burdened with sins and swayed by various impulses, ⁷who will listen to anybody and can never arrive at a knowledge of the truth. ⁸As Jannes and Jambres opposed Moses, so these men also oppose the truth, men of corrupt mind and counterfeit faith; ⁹but they will not get very far, for their folly will be plain to all, as was that of those two men.

The rest of this first paragraph of chapter 3 is devoted to a thorough portrayal of these men. In particular, Paul delineates their moral conduct (2–4), their religious observance (5) and their proselytizing zeal (6–9).

a. Their moral conduct (verses 2–4)

In these three verses the apostle employs no fewer than nineteen expressions by which to describe the wicked men who are responsible for the 'times of stress'. It might perhaps be a little tedious to analyse the portrait too minutely and to define each term separately. But notice at once the first and the last phrases used. The first says that they are 'lovers of self' (*philautoi*) and the last (4) that they are not, as they should be, 'lovers of God' (*philotheoi*). Indeed four of the nineteen expressions are compounded with 'love' (*phil-*), suggesting that what is fundamentally wrong with these people is that their love is misdirected. Instead of being first and foremost 'lovers of God', they are 'lovers of self', 'lovers of money' (NEB: 'men will love nothing but money and self') and 'lovers of pleasure' (4).

In between these four come fifteen other expressions, which are almost entirely descriptive of the breakdown of men's relations with each other.

The first three enlarge on the meaning of self-love. People

who love themselves best become 'proud', 'arrogant' and 'abusive'. The first word means 'braggarts' or 'swashbucklers' (*alazones*), and the second 'haughty' or 'disdainful' (*hyperēphanoi*) which leads naturally to the third 'slanderous' (*blasphēmoi*), because inevitably those who have an exaggerated opinion of themselves look down with contempt upon others and speak evil of them.

The next five words may conveniently be grouped together. For they seem to refer to family life, and especially to the attitude which some young people adopt towards their parents. The Greek words are all negative in form and begin with the prefix *a-*, like our English words beginning un- or dis-, as if to stress the tragic absence of qualities which nature alone would lead one to expect. The first two are 'disobedient to their parents', whom Scripture says children are to honour and—at least during their minority—obey, and 'ungrateful', devoid of even an elementary appreciation. The next word is translated 'unholy' (*anosioi*), for *hosios* normally means 'devout' or 'pious' towards God. But like the similar adjective *eusebēs* ('reverent') it was sometimes used in classical Greek of filial respect. The context suggests that this may be the allusion here. 'Inhuman' (*astorgoi*) is rendered by JBP 'utterly lacking in . . . normal human affections' and by RSV in Romans 1:31 'heartless', because it is part of the natural, created order that parents and children should love each other. The last word of this group of five is 'implacable' (*aspondoi*) and is translated by AG 'irreconcilable'. It describes a situation in which people (maybe the reference is still primarily to young people) are so much in revolt that they are not even willing to come to the conference table to negotiate. In an ideal society the relationship of children to their parents should be marked by obedience, gratitude, respect, affection and reasonableness. In 'times of stress' all five are lacking.

The remaining seven words of the catalogue are obviously wider than the family. The first is 'slanderers' (*diaboloi*, literally 'devils'), translated 'backbiters' by E. K. Simpson and 'scandalmongers' in NEB. They are guilty of the sin of speaking evil against others, especially behind their back. They are also 'profligates' (*akrateis*), 'ungovernable' (Simpson) or lacking in self-control, 'fierce' (*anēmeroi*) or 'untamed' (AG), and 'haters of good' (*aphilagathoi*) or 'strangers to all goodness' (NEB). Finally, they are 'treacherous' (a word used in Luke 6:16 of the traitor Judas), 'reckless' (entirely thoughtless in word and deed) and 'swollen with conceit' or 'puffed up' (connoting 'self-importance, bumptiousness'[1]). Thus we are back to the basic evil with which the hideous list began, namely pride.

And all this unsocial, anti-social behaviour—this disobedient, ungrateful, disrespectful, inhuman attitude to parents, together with this absence of restraint, loyalty, prudence and humility—is the inevitable consequence of a godless self-centredness. Archbishop Trench, commenting on the meaning of *philautos*, 'selfish', mentions an unnamed Puritan divine who 'likens the selfish man to the hedgehog which, rolling itself up in a ball, presents only sharp spines to those without, keeping at the same time all the soft and warm wool for itself within'.[2] If a man is 'proud', 'arrogant' and 'swollen with conceit', of course he will never sacrifice himself to serve others. God's order, as plainly declared in his moral law, is that we love him first (with all our heart, soul, mind and strength), our neighbour next and our self last. If we reverse the order of the first and third, putting self first and God last, our neighbour in the middle is bound to suffer.

So the root of the trouble in 'times of stress' is that men are 'utterly self-centred' (JBP), 'lovers of self' (*philautoi*), 'an Aristotelian term . . . for inordinate self-love'.[3]

Only the gospel offers a radical solution to this problem. For only the gospel promises a new birth or new creation, which involves being turned inside out, from self to unself, a real reorientation of mind and conduct, and which makes us fundamentally God-centred instead of self-centred. Then, when God is first and self is last, we love the world God loves and seek to give and serve like him.

b. *Their religious observance* (verse 5)

It may be a shock to discover that people such as these, who lack the common decencies of civilized society let alone of God's

[1] Simpson, p. 144.
[2] *Synonyms of the New Testament* by R. C. Trench, 1854. 9th edition 1880, xciii, p. 329.
[3] Simpson, p. 143.

law, can also be religious. But it is true. In the history of mankind, although this is a shameful thing to confess, religion and morality have been more often divorced than married. Certainly Scripture bears an unwavering testimony to this fact. The great ethical prophets of the 7th and 8th centuries BC fulminated against Israel and Judah on this score. Amos was the first, exposing the anomaly that in the reign of Jeroboam II there was a boom in religion and in injustice simultaneously. Israelite worshippers 'lay themselves down beside every altar upon garments taken in pledge', he cried; 'and in the house of their God they drink the wine of those who have been fined (*sc.* unjustly)' (Am. 2:8). In other words, in the very performance of their religious duties they were making use of garments and wine to which they had no moral right. Their immorality had actually invaded their religious observance.

Isaiah deplored the same thing in Judah. Through him God addressed his people thus:

'Your new moons and your appointed feasts
   my soul hates;
they have become a burden to me,
   I am weary of bearing them.
When you spread forth your hands,
   I will hide my eyes from you;
even though you make many prayers,
   I will not listen;
   your hands are full of blood.
Wash yourselves; make yourselves clean;
   remove the evil of your doings
   from before my eyes;
cease to do evil,
   learn to do good;
seek justice,
   correct oppression;
defend the fatherless,
   plead for the widow' (Is. 1:14–17).

The Lord Jesus had to utter a very similar complaint against the Pharisees, the ultra-religious people of his day: 'you cleanse the outside of the cup and of the plate, but inside they are full of extortion and rapacity' (Mt. 23:25). That is, they were meticulous in ensuring the ceremonial purity of their vessels, while what they ate and drank from their clean vessels had been acquired by unclean greed and dishonesty.

Still the same malady was rife among the people Paul is describing. They preserved the outward 'form of religion' but were 'denying the power of it' (5). They evidently attended the worship services of the church. They sang the hymns, said the 'amen' to the prayers and put their money in the offering-plate. They looked and sounded egregiously pious. But it was *form* without *power*, outward show without inward reality, religion without morals, faith without works.

True religion combines form and power. It is not external form without power. Nor, on the other hand, does it emphasize moral power in such a way as to despise or dispense with proper external forms. It combines them. It fosters a worship which is essentially 'spiritual', arising from the heart, but which expresses itself through public, corporate services, and which also issues in moral behaviour. Otherwise, it is not only valueless; it is actually an abomination to the Lord.

No wonder Paul adds: 'avoid such people'. Not that he was to avoid all contact with sinners, for Jesus himself had been 'the friend of publicans and sinners', and if Timothy were to shun association with them he would have to go right out of the world (*cf.* 1 Cor. 5:9–12). Paul means rather that within the church, for he has been giving a description of 'a kind of heathen Christianity',[1] Timothy was to have nothing to do with what might be called 'religious sinners'. Indeed, one could go further. Anybody whom the Book of Common Prayer terms 'an open and notorious evil liver' should be disciplined, and, if he remains unrepentant, excommunicated (*cf.* 1 Cor. 5:5, 13).

c. Their proselytizing zeal (verses 6–9)

It is indeed astonishing that the kind of people the apostle has been describing, filled with godless self-love and malice, should not only profess religion, but include some who actively propagate it. Yet such was the case.

[1] Ellicott, p. 144.

It seems probable that their proselytizing zeal is portrayed as a military operation. The verb translated 'capture' (*aichmalōtizō*) properly means to take prisoner in war, although AG add that 'the figure may fade' so that the word comes to signify 'carry away = mislead, deceive'. At all events, their method was not direct and open, but furtive, secretive, cunning. They were sneaks. Using no doubt the back door rather than the front, these tradesmen of heresy would insinuate themselves into private homes or 'households'. Choosing a time when the menfolk were out (presumably at work), they concentrated their attention on 'weak women'. This expedient, comments Bishop Ellicott, was 'as old as the fall of man',[1] for the serpent first deceived Eve. It was also employed by the Gnostics, and has been the regular ploy of religious commercial travellers right up to and including the Jehovah's Witnesses of our own day.

The women chosen as victims Paul refers to by the word *gynaikaria*, 'little women', a term of contempt for women who were idle, silly and weak. Their weakness was double. First, they were morally weak, 'burdened with sins and swayed by various impulses'. Their sins were to them both a burden and a tyrant, and the false teachers, worming their way into their home, played upon their feelings of guilt and of infirmity. Secondly, they were intellectually weak, unstable, credulous, gullible. They were the kind of women who would 'listen to anybody', while at the same time they could 'never arrive at a knowledge of the truth'. Constitutionally incapable of reaching any settled convictions, they were like little boats tossed hither and thither by a storm (*cf*. Eph. 4:14). In such a state of mental confusion, people will listen to any teacher, however specious. 'It was no love of truth that impelled them to learn,' however, 'but only a morbid love of novelty.'[2] Such women, weak in character and intellect, are an easy prey for door-to-door religious salesmen.

As an example of spurious teachers Paul now mentions 'Jannes and Jambres', the names (according to Jewish tradition) of the two chief magicians in Pharaoh's court. They are not named in the Old Testament text, although one of the Targums inserts their names in Exodus 7:11 which reads: 'Then Pharaoh summoned the wise men and the sorcerers; and they also, the

[1] Ellicott, p. 146.   [2] Ellicott, p. 146.

magicians of Egypt, did the same (*sc.* miracles) by their secret arts.'

The implication of what Paul writes here is extremely important, although it does not lie on the surface. He draws a historical parallel between Jannes and Jambres who had opposed Moses centuries previously and 'these men' (the false teachers of his own day) who also oppose the truth. Jannes and Jambres were magicians; the false teachers also were 'impostors' and 'deceivers' (13). Perhaps they too went in for magic of some kind, for when the Ephesians who had 'practised magic arts' were converted, they had brought their books and publicly burned them (Acts 19:18, 19). What is remarkable about this analogy, however, is not just that the Asian false teachers are likened to the Egyptian magicians but that Paul is thereby likening himself to Moses! For Moses was the greatest figure of the Old Testament. No prophet arose like him in Israel, we are told, either in his knowledge of God ('whom the Lord knew face to face') or in the signs and wonders he did to authenticate the revelation of God (Dt. 34:10, 11). 'See,' the Lord had said to him, 'I make you as God to Pharaoh . . . You shall speak all that I command you' (Ex. 7:1, 2). So for forty years Moses spoke God's word and gave God's law to the people.

But now Paul dares to equate himself with Moses. For as Jannes and Jambres opposed Moses, so the Asian false teachers were opposing the truth. What truth? Why, the truth taught by Paul and entrusted by Paul to Timothy (1:14), the apostolic faith, the sacred deposit, which Timothy was to guard and to transmit. Thus the apostle Paul, naturally and without any apparent hesitation, puts himself on a level with Moses as one who also taught God's truth. Moses taught the law; Paul preached the gospel. But whether it was law or gospel, the teaching of Moses the prophet or Paul the apostle, it was God's truth which men were opposing and rejecting.

So Paul rejects them as men who were 'corrupt' in their 'mind', despite their claim to *gnōsis* (knowledge), and 'counterfeit' (*adokimoi*, 'tried and found wanting') as to their 'faith'. Moreover he is confident that such men 'will not get very far'. They may themselves 'go on from bad to worse' (13). Their false teaching may also temporarily spread and 'eat its way like gangrene' (2:17).

But its success will be limited and transient. How could Paul be so sure? Because 'their folly will be plain to all, as was (or 'came to be' *egeneto*, an aorist) that of those two men', Jannes and Jambres.

We sometimes get distressed in our day—rightly and understandably—by the false teachers who oppose the truth and trouble the church, especially by the sly and slippery methods of backdoor religious traders. But we need have no fear, even if a few weak people may be taken in, even if falsehood becomes fashionable. For there is something patently spurious about heresy, and something self-evidently true about the truth. Error may spread and be popular for a time. But it 'will not get very far'. In the end it is bound to be exposed, and the truth is sure to be vindicated. This is a clear lesson of church history. Numerous heresies have arisen, and some have seemed likely to triumph. But today they are largely of antiquarian interest. God has preserved his truth in the church.

Having reached the end of the first paragraph of chapter 3, it should now be plain to us what these dangerous seasons are which occur spasmodically in 'the last days' in which we live, and how they arise. It is because in that part of God's field (the world) in which God has sown wheat, the devil has also sown weeds.[1] Changing the image, the devil has his 'fifth column', his secret agents, actually inside the church. As the Church of England's *Article XXVI* puts it: 'in the visible Church the evil (is) ever mingled with the good, and sometimes the evil have chief authority in the Ministration of the Word and Sacraments . . .' Yes, inside the church, within the visible society of professing believers, there are men of immoral character and conduct, of purely external religiosity, of corrupt mind and counterfeit faith. They are lovers of self, money and pleasure rather than lovers of God and their fellows. They retain the form of religion but deny its power. They oppose the truth and seek to win the weak to their pernicious errors. Morally, religiously and intellectually they are perverse. It is a remarkably apt portrayal of the so-called 'permissive society', which genially tolerates every conceivable deviation from Christian standards of righteousness and truth, and whose ethos has crept into the church.

[1] *Cf.* Jesus' parable recorded in Mt. 13:24-30, 36-43.

But Timothy is not to catch this infection, nor be carried away by this flood-tide, but to stand out boldly against the prevailing fashion.

3. STANDING FIRM IN THE FAITH (verses 10–15)

Now you have observed my teaching, my conduct, my aim in life, my faith, my patience, my love, my steadfastness, 11 my persecutions, my sufferings, what befell me at Antioch, at Iconium, and at Lystra, what persecutions I endured; yet from them all the Lord rescued me. 12 Indeed all who desire to live a godly life in Christ Jesus will be persecuted, 13 while evil men and impostors will go on from bad to worse, deceivers and deceived. 14 But as for you, continue in what you have learned and have firmly believed, knowing from whom you learned it 15 and how from childhood you have been acquainted with the sacred writings which are able to instruct you for salvation through faith in Christ Jesus.

In this paragraph Paul twice addresses Timothy with the same two little Greek monosyllables *su de*. They come at the beginning of verses 10 and 14 (like the *su oun* of 2:1) and should be translated 'But as for you . . .'. In stark contrast to the contemporary decline in morals, empty show of religion and spread of false teaching Timothy is called to be different, and if necessary to stand alone.

Every Christian is called to be different from the world. 'Don't let the world around you squeeze you into its own mould' (Rom. 12:2, JBP). Certainly the pressures upon us to conform are colossal, not only from the direct challenge to traditional beliefs and morals, but also—and more—from the insidious, pervasive atmosphere of secularism which even seeps into the church. Many give in, often without realizing what they are doing. But again and again the word of God addresses us, calling us not to be moved. We are not to be like a 'reed shaken with the wind', feebly bowing down before it from whatever direction it may blow. Rather, like a rock in a mountain torrent, we are to stand firm.

One might paraphrase the apostle's double exhortation to Timothy in verses 10 to 14 like this: 'But as for you, in spite of all the current false teaching, what you have been closely following is *my* doctrine and *my* way of life, together with *my* purpose, faith, patience, love, endurance, persecutions and sufferings ... Wicked men and charlatans, deceiving others and themselves deceived, will still make their strange progress from bad to worse. But as for you, you are not to progress in any direction, least of all away from or beyond my teaching (for that would be declension, not advance). On the contrary, you are to stand firm, to continue and abide in what you learned and have believed, because you know from whom you learned it ...'

Paul first reminds Timothy what he has been doing thus far: 'you have observed' or followed 'my teaching' (10). Then he exhorts him to continue in the same path: 'continue in what you have learned' (14). So verses 10 to 13 describe Timothy's *past* loyalty to the apostle, and verses 14 to 17 urge him to remain loyal in the *future*. The two main verbs sum up the gist of the paragraph: 'you have *followed* me faithfully up till now (10); so then *continue* to do so (14)'.

a. The past (verses 10–13)

Timothy's position is explained in terms of a certain 'following' of Paul. The verb *parakoloutheō* can be used literally, of following a person as he goes somewhere and of walking in his footsteps. But it is not so used in the New Testament. Its figurative use can refer either to an intellectual following, much as we say to a person who is explaining something to us 'I follow you', or to a real commitment of mind and life as when we say of somebody 'he's a follower of So-and-so'. AG define these two meanings as to 'follow with the mind, understand, make one's own' and to 'follow faithfully, follow as a rule'. Luke uses the verb more or less in the former sense, when he tells Theophilus of his painstaking historical investigations. He has 'followed all things closely for some time past', he writes (Lk. 1:3). But Paul seems to use the verb in the other and more committed sense in his letters to Timothy. In the first letter he has urged Timothy to nourish himself on 'the good doctrine which you have followed', that is, embraced. So surely the verb has the same meaning here in the second letter. Paul is reminding Timothy not simply that he has 'fully known' (AV) or 'observed' (RSV) his doctrine and conduct, as if he were merely an impartial student or a detached observer, but that he has become a dedicated disciple of the apostle's. No doubt he had begun by taking pains to grasp the meaning of Paul's instruction. But then he went further. He made it his own, believed it, absorbed it, lived by it. Similarly, he doubtless began by watching the apostle's manner of life, but then he went on to imitate it. Because Paul knew himself as an apostle to be following Christ, he did not hesitate to invite others to follow himself: 'Be imitators of me,' he wrote, 'as I am of Christ' (1 Cor. 11:1; *cf.* 1 Thes. 1:6). He even made himself the standard by which truth could be distinguished from falsehood: 'Brethren, join in imitating me, and mark those who so live as you have an example in us' (Phil. 3:17). Thus, in both belief and practice, in 'teaching' and 'conduct' (10), Timothy became and remained Paul's faithful follower. He had 'followed step by step' (NEB).

The contrast with the first paragraph of this chapter is obvious. The men described there were following their own inclinations (they were lovers of self, money and pleasure), and their pathetic converts had been carried away by their own impulses. Timothy, on the other hand, has followed an altogether different standard, namely the teaching and the example of Christ's apostle Paul. So Paul goes on to list the characteristics of his life, in contrast to that of the self-lovers whom he has characterized in verses 2–5. The emphatic words are the personal pronouns and possessive adjectives. They bring out the contrast clearly: 'For men will be lovers of self . . . *They* will be and do this and that. But as for *you*, Timothy, *you* (as distinct from *them*) have followed *me*, *my* teaching, *my* conduct, *etc.*'

Why, however, does Paul give us in verses 10 and 11 this catalogue of his virtues and sufferings? Is it not more than a little immodest, even conceited, that the apostle should put himself forward like this? Perhaps it is understandable that he should mention his 'teaching', but why go on to blow his own trumpet about his faith and love, his purpose and conduct, his sufferings and his endurance? Is it not rather unseemly that he should boast like this?

No, Paul is not boasting. He has reasons quite other than exhibitionism for drawing attention to himself. He mentions his teaching first, and then goes on to supply two objective evidences of the genuineness of his teaching, namely the life he lived and the sufferings he endured. Indeed, these are good (though not infallible) general tests of a person's sincerity, and even of the truth or falsehood of his system. Is he so convinced of his position that he both practises what he preaches and is prepared to suffer for it? Have his beliefs made him a better man, even in the face of opposition? Paul could answer both questions affirmatively. The false teachers lived lives of self-indulgence, and it would be quite out of character to expect them to be willing to suffer for their views; they were altogether too soft and easy-going for that. The apostle Paul, however, lived a consistent life of righteousness, self-control, faith and love, and remained steadfast to his principles through many and grievous persecutions.

Look at his behaviour first. Timothy had observed and tried to imitate Paul's 'conduct' (*agōgē*, his whole demeanour and way of life), his 'aim in life' (the spiritual ambitions which motivated him and made life meaningful for him), his 'faith' (which perhaps here includes his fidelity), his 'patience' (*makrothymia*, tolerance or long-suffering towards aggravating people), his 'love' (towards both God and man, as opposed to the false teachers' love for self, money and pleasure) and his 'steadfastness' (*hypomonē*, the patient endurance of trying circumstances, in distinction to *makrothymia*, the patient endurance of trying people). Indeed, since *hypomonē* ('steadfastness') is regularly in the New Testament the child of our Christian 'hope', our expectation of the Lord's return and the glory to follow, we may detect within this list yet another example of Paul's favourite triad of graces 'faith, hope and love'.[1]

The reference to 'steadfastness' or 'endurance' naturally leads on to the 'persecutions' and the 'sufferings' which Paul had had to endure. In particular, he mentions the three Galatian cities Antioch, Iconium and Lystra, because Timothy was a citizen of Lystra and had possibly himself witnessed the occasion when the apostle had been stoned by a hostile mob, dragged out of the city and left in the gutter for dead, though from this and all other persecutions so far the Lord had rescued him. Perhaps Paul's

[1] See 1 Cor. 13:13; Col. 1:4, 5; 1 Thes. 1:3; 2 Thes. 1:3, 4; *cf.* Heb. 10:22–24.

courage under persecution had even played a part in Timothy's conversion, much as Stephen's bravery in martyrdom had done in Paul's. At all events, Timothy had 'followed' Paul's persecutions, first watching them, and then discovering that he must himself share in them, for he could not be committed to Paul's teaching and conduct without becoming involved in his sufferings also.[1]

In verse 12 Paul makes it clear that his experience was not unique. He sought to live 'a godly life in Christ Jesus', loving and serving God rather than himself, and he suffered for it. Timothy had found the same thing. For all Christian people who 'in Christ Jesus' (*i.e.* through union with him) 'desire to live a godly life . . . will be persecuted', and indeed are bound to suffer persecution. The godly arouse the antagonism of the worldly. It has always been so. It was so for Christ, and he said it would be for us: 'If the world hates you, know that it has hated me before it hated you. If you were of the world, the world would love its own; but because you are not of the world, but I chose you out of the world, therefore the world hates you. Remember the word that I said to you, "A servant is not greater than his master." If they have persecuted me, they will persecute you' (Jn. 15:18–20; *cf.* 16:33). It is important to notice the situation in which Christ here told his followers to expect persecution. He envisaged that they would be both in the world (living among godless people) and at the same time 'not of the world' (living a godly life in Christ). Those who are in Christ but not in the world are not persecuted, because they do not come into contact and therefore into collision with their potential persecutors. Those who are in the world but not in Christ are also not persecuted, because the world sees nothing in them to persecute. The former escape persecution by withdrawal from the world, the latter by assimilation to it. It is only for those who are both in the world and in Christ simultaneously that persecution becomes inevitable. As Calvin comments, 'it is in vain to try to detach Christ from his cross, and it is only natural that the world should hate Christ even in his members'.[2]

[1] See Acts 13:14–14:23 for the Galatian cities Paul visited on his first missionary journey, and for the persecutions he endured there.

[2] Calvin, p. 327.

This inevitability of persecution is further explained in verse 13 by the continued activities of false teachers. Paul is quite outspoken about them. He dubs them 'evil men' and 'impostors'. The latter word (*goēs*) means a 'sorcerer, juggler' and so in early Christian literature a 'swindler, cheat' (AG). The apostle does not credit them with sincerity; they are 'charlatans' (NEB). Such men 'will go on from bad to worse'. The verb for 'go on' (*prokoptō*) properly means to 'go forward, progress', but here Paul uses it ironically, since the only advance they make is backwards, not forwards, 'from bad to worse'. He appears to be referring not to their success as teachers, for he has said that 'they will not get very far' (9), but to their own personal deterioration, both intellectual and moral. They are 'deceivers and deceived'. Alfred Plummer explains it well: 'they begin by being seducers and end in being dupes, and the dupes (very often) of their own deceptions; for deceit commonly leads to self-deceit'.[1]

b. The future (verses 14, 15)

So far in this paragraph Paul has been describing himself, but doing so in relation to Timothy who has taken him as his guide. Timothy is seen to stand out in bold relief against the background of the prevalent evildoers and false teachers. For he has carefully 'followed' Paul and modelled himself on Paul's teaching. Moreover, he has been right to do so, for Paul's teaching has been amply confirmed by his godly life and by his many persecutions bravely borne. Now for the second time Paul begins a sentence 'But as for you' (*su de*), distinguishing Timothy from the 'evil men and impostors' he has just described. Previously he has contrasted their pursuit of their own inclinations with Timothy's faithful following of apostolic doctrine and example. Now he draws another contrast: they 'go on' (though we have seen what a peculiar form their progress assumed), whereas Timothy is to 'continue' or abide in what he has learned and believed.

This kind of summons is not infrequently heard in the pages of the New Testament. It is specially relevant whenever innovators arise in the church, 'radicals' who claim to be progressive and who repudiate everything which savours of the traditional.

[1] Plummer, p. 385.

It has perhaps never been more needed than today when men boast of inventing a 'new Christianity' with a 'new theology' and a 'new morality', all of which betoken a 'new reformation'. To be sure, the church of every generation must seek to translate the faith into the contemporary idiom, to relate the unchanging word to the changing world. But a translation is a rendering of the same message into another language; it is not a fresh composition. Yet this is what some modern radicals are doing, setting forth concepts of God and of Christ which Jesus and his apostles would not have recognized as their own. In such a situation we may perhaps be forgiven if, borrowing the Lord's own words, we say to them: 'no one after drinking old wine desires new; for he says, "the old is better" ' (Lk. 5:39, RSV mg.). The apostles themselves constantly warned their readers of newfangled ideas and called them back to the original apostolic message. Thus John declares that 'anyone who goes ahead and does not *abide* in the doctrine of Christ does not have God' and exhorts his flock 'let what you heard from the beginning *abide* in you', for then they would '*abide* in the Son and in the Father' (2 Jn. 9; 1 Jn. 2:24). Similarly here Paul enjoins Timothy to *abide* in what he has learned. In each of these verses the Greek verb is the same. Timothy had learned things and now firmly believed them. All right. Now he must *continue* in these things with steadfastness and not allow anyone to shift him from his ground.

The apostle now adds two reasons. His clear command to Timothy to abide, to cultivate stability in the truths he has learned, rests on two simple and plain arguments which he elaborates in verses 14b and 15. Timothy must continue in *what* he has learned, because he knows from *whom* he has learned it. The teaching was guaranteed by the teacher. And who was this? The Greek manuscripts have two readings, one making 'whom' plural and the other singular. The better attested is the plural (*para tinōn*), in which case the teachers referred to will include his grandmother Lois and his mother Eunice (who had indeed taught him from his infancy; see 1:5; 3:15) as well as the apostle Paul. Commentators who weigh the manuscript evidence go no further than to say that this reading is 'perhaps to be preferred'[1] or is 'probably correct'.[2] They agree that the alternative (the

---

[1] Ellicott, p. 152.   [2] Barrett, p. 113.

singular *para tinos*) is also well attested, however, and this would refer to the apostle Paul alone. Although the external authority for this reading is slightly less strong, the internal evidence seems to me to be more strongly in its favour. That is to say, in the immediate context Paul has been placing emphasis on the fact that Timothy has closely followed his teaching (10). That Paul's apostolic instruction was Timothy's model is stressed by the emphatic 'my' and 'me' of verses 10 and 11.

The wider context of the whole letter points the same way. In the first two chapters, the apostle has begged Timothy both to 'follow the pattern of the sound words *which you have heard from me*' (1:13) and then to entrust to others '*what you have heard from me*' (2:2). It seems probable, therefore, that the phrase 'knowing from whom you learned it' in 3:14 also refers to what Timothy has heard from Paul. Besides, the apostle is apparently giving *two* reasons for Timothy's continued loyalty; it is likely, therefore, that these will be distinct reasons and not both refer to his childhood education in the Scriptures.

In this case, the first ground of Timothy's confidence, and the first reason why he should continue in what he has learned is that he has learned it from Paul. And he knows this Paul who has taught him. He has not only led him to Christ (1:2) and laid hands on him at his ordination (1:6), but he is also 'an apostle of Jesus Christ by the will of God' (1:1), to whom Christ had entrusted the deposit of the gospel (1:11, 12), who has likened himself to Moses in his teaching of the truth (3:8), whose doctrine and example Timothy has loyally followed thus far, and who has confirmed his teaching by his consistent life and his fortitude in persecution. Timothy was confident in Paul and his teaching authority, and we can share his confidence. Paul's gospel is still authenticated to us by his apostolic authority.

Timothy has not only learned Paul's gospel and known Paul's authority. 'From childhood' he had been instructed in the Old Testament Scriptures presumably by his mother and grandmother, and he was therefore extremely familiar with them. He believed them to be divinely inspired, as Paul is about to say. So the second reason why he must abide in what he has learned from Paul is its harmony with these very Scriptures. This was Paul's consistent claim. On trial before King Agrippa he had affirmed that he was teaching 'nothing but what the prophets and Moses said would come to pass; that the Christ must suffer, and that, by being the first to rise from the dead, he would proclaim light both to the people and to the Gentiles' (Acts 26:22, 23). Similarly, at the beginning of his letter to the Romans he had described God's gospel to which he was set apart as what God had 'promised beforehand through his prophets in the holy scriptures' (Rom. 1:2; *cf*. 3:21).

So then, the two reasons why Timothy should remain loyal to what he has come firmly to believe are that he has learned it both from Old Testament Scripture and from the apostle Paul. The same two grounds apply today. The gospel we believe is the biblical gospel, the gospel of the Old Testament and of the New Testament, vouched for by both the prophets of God and the apostles of Christ. And we must resolve ourselves to heed the exhortation which Paul addressed to Timothy and to abide in what we have learned because of this double authentication.

4. THE ORIGIN AND PURPOSE OF SCRIPTURE
(verses 15b–17)

... the sacred writings which are able to instruct you for salvation through faith in Christ Jesus. [16] *All scripture is inspired by God and profitable for teaching, for reproof, for correction, and for training in righteousness,* [17] *that the man of God may be complete, equipped for every good work.*

Two fundamental truths about Scripture are asserted here. The first concerns its origin (where it comes from) and the second its purpose (what it is intended for).

First, 'All scripture is inspired by God'; it is God-breathed. Some scholars, as in NEB, have translated the opening words of verse 16: 'every inspired Scripture has its use'. Such a rendering would place a double limitation on Scripture. It would suggest that not all Scripture is inspired, and that therefore not all Scripture is profitable, but only those parts which are inspired. Since the Greek sentence has no main verb, it is certainly legitimate, grammatically speaking, to supply the verb 'is' after, rather than before, the adjective 'God-inspired' and so translate 'every God-inspired Scripture is profitable'. The argument against this construction, however, is that it does not do justice to the little word 'and' (*kai*) which comes between the two adjectives 'God-inspired' and 'profitable'. This 'and' suggests that Paul is asserting two truths about Scripture, namely that it is both inspired *and* profitable, not merely one. For this reason we should render the sentence: 'all Scripture is God-inspired and profitable'.

What does he mean by 'all Scripture'? It seems to me not at all impossible that by this comprehensive expression he is including the two sources of Timothy's knowledge just mentioned, namely 'what you have learned' (*sc.* from me) and 'the sacred writings'. It is true that nowhere does the apostle explicitly call his Epistles 'Scripture'. Nevertheless, on a number of occasions he gets very near it, and he certainly directs that his letters be read publicly in the Christian assemblies, no doubt alongside Old Testament readings (*e.g.* Col. 4:16; 1 Thes. 5:27). Several times he claims to be speaking in the name and with the authority of Christ (*e.g.* 2 Cor. 2:17; 13:3; Gal. 4:14), and calls his message 'the word of God' (*e.g.* 1 Thes. 2:13). Once he says that, in communicating to others what God has revealed to him, he uses 'words not taught by human wisdom but taught by the Spirit' (1 Cor. 2:13). This is a claim to inspiration, indeed to verbal inspiration, which is the distinctive characteristic of 'Scripture'. Peter clearly regarded Paul's letters as Scripture, for in referring to them he calls the Old Testament 'the other scriptures' (2 Pet. 3:16). In addition, it seems evident that Paul envisaged the possibility of a Christian supplement to the Old Testament because he could combine a quotation from Deuteronomy (25:4) with a saying of Jesus recorded by Luke (10:7) and call both alike 'Scripture' (1 Tim. 5:18).

His definition of Scripture, of 'all scripture', is that it is 'inspired by God'. The single Greek word *theopneustos* would be literally translated 'God-breathed' and indicates not that Scripture itself or its human authors were breathed into by God, but that Scripture was breathed or breathed out by God. 'Inspiration' is doubtless a convenient term to use, but 'spiration' or even 'expiration' would convey the meaning of the Greek adjective more accurately. Scripture is not to be thought of as already in existence when (subsequently) God breathed into it, but as itself brought into existence by the breath or Spirit of God. There is no 'theory' or explanation of inspiration here, for no reference is made to the human authors, who (Peter says) 'moved by the Holy Spirit spoke from God' (2 Pet. 1:21). Nevertheless, it is clear from many passages that inspiration, however the process operated, did not destroy the individuality or the active co-operation of the human writers. All that is stated here is the fact of inspiration, that all Scripture is God-breathed. It originated in God's mind and was communicated from God's mouth by God's breath or Spirit. It is therefore rightly termed 'the Word of God', for God spoke it. Indeed, as the prophets used to say, 'the mouth of the Lord has spoken it'.

Secondly, Paul explains the purpose of Scripture: it is 'profit-able'. And this is precisely because it is inspired by God. Only its divine origin secures and explains its human profit. In order to show what this is, Paul uses two expressions. The first is in verse 15: 'The sacred writings', he says, 'are able to instruct you for salvation.' The Bible is essentially a handbook of salvation. Its over-arching purpose is to teach not facts of science (*e.g.* the nature of moon rock) which men can discover by their own empirical investigation, but facts of salvation, which no space exploration can discover but only God can reveal. The whole Bible unfolds the divine scheme of salvation—man's creation in God's image, his fall through disobedience into sin and under judgment, God's continuing love for him in spite of his rebellion, God's eternal plan to save him through his covenant of grace with a chosen people, culminating in Christ; the coming of Christ as the Saviour, who died to bear man's sin, was raised from death, was exalted to heaven and sent the Holy Spirit; and man's rescue first from guilt and alienation, then from bondage, and finally from mortality in his progressive experience of the liberty of God's children. None of this would be known apart from the biblical revelation. 'Scripture contains the perfect rule of a good and happy life.'[1]

More particularly, the Bible instructs for salvation 'through

[1] Calvin, p. 330.

faith in Christ Jesus'. So, since the Bible is a book of salvation, and since salvation is through Christ, the Bible focuses its attention upon Christ. The Old Testament foretells and foreshadows him in many and various ways; the Gospels tell the story of his birth and life, his words and works, his death and resurrection; the Acts describe what he continued to do and teach through his chosen apostles, especially in spreading the gospel and establishing the church from Jerusalem to Rome; the Epistles display the full glory of his person and work, and apply it to the life of the Christian and the church; while the Revelation depicts Christ sharing the throne of God now and coming soon to consummate his salvation and judgment. This comprehensive portraiture of Jesus Christ is intended to elicit our 'faith' in him, in order that by faith we may be saved.

Paul now goes on to show that the profit of Scripture relates to both creed and conduct (16b, 17). The false teachers divorced them; we must marry them. The NEB expresses the matter clearly. As for our creed, Scripture is profitable 'for teaching the truth and refuting error'. As for our conduct, it is profitable 'for reformation of manners and discipline in right living'. In each pair the negative and positive counterparts are combined. Do we hope, either in our own lives or in our teaching ministry, to overcome error and grow in truth, to overcome evil and grow in holiness? Then it is to Scripture that we must primarily turn, for Scripture is 'profitable' for these things.

Indeed, Scripture is the chief means which God employs to bring 'the man of God' to maturity. Who is intended by this expression is not explained. It may be a general term for every Christian, since the words themselves mean no more than 'the man who belongs to God' (NEB). On the other hand, it was an Old Testament title of respect applied to some of God's spokesmen like Moses (Dt. 33:1), David (2 Ch. 8:14) and Elijah (1 Ki. 17:18), and Paul specifically addressed Timothy by this phrase in his first letter (6:11). It may therefore refer here to men called to positions of responsibility in the church, and especially to ministers whose task it is, under the authority of Scripture, to teach and refute, to reform and discipline. At all events, it is only by a diligent study of Scripture that the man of God may become 'complete, equipped for every good work'.

Looking back over this chapter as a whole, we can appreciate the relevance of its message to our pluralist and permissive society. The 'times of stress' in which we seem to be living are very distressing. Sometimes one wonders if the world and the church have gone mad, so strange are their views, and so lax their standards. Some Christians are swept from their moorings by the floodtide of sin and error. Others go into hiding, as offering the best hope of survival, the only alternative to surrender. But neither of these is the Christian way. 'But as for you,' Paul says to us as he did to Timothy, 'stand firm. Never mind if the pressure to conform is very strong. Never mind if you are young, inexperienced, timid and weak. Never mind if you find yourself alone in your witness. You have followed my teaching so far. Now continue in what you have come to believe. You know the biblical credentials of your faith. Scripture is God-breathed and profitable. Even in the midst of these grievous times in which evil men and impostors go on from bad to worse, it can make you complete and it can equip you for your work. Let the word of God make you a man of God! Remain loyal to it and it will lead you on into Christian maturity.'

Chapter 4

THE CHARGE TO PREACH THE GOSPEL

THIS chapter contains some of the very last words spoken or written by the apostle Paul. They are certainly the last which have survived. He is writing within weeks, perhaps even within days, of his martyrdom. According to a fairly reliable tradition he was beheaded on the Ostian Way. For about 30 years without intermission he has laboured as an apostle and an itinerant evangelist. Truly, as he himself here writes, he has fought a good fight, finished his course and kept the faith (7). Now he awaits his reward, 'the crown of righteousness' which has been laid up for him in heaven (8). So these words are Paul's legacy to the church. They breathe an atmosphere of great solemnity. It is impossible to read them without being profoundly stirred.

The early part of the chapter takes the form of an impressive charge. 'I charge you in the presence of God,' he begins. The verb *diamartyromai* has legal connections and can mean to 'testify under oath' in a court of law or to 'adjure' a witness to do so. It is used in the New Testament of any 'solemn and emphatic utterance' (MM). Paul's charge is addressed in the first instance to Timothy, his apostolic delegate and representative in Ephesus. But it is applicable in a secondary sense to every man called to an evangelistic or pastoral ministry, even to all Christian people.

There are three aspects of the charge to be studied, namely its nature (precisely what Paul is commissioning Timothy to do), its basis (the arguments on which Paul grounds his charge) and a personal illustration of it from Paul's own example in Rome.

1. THE NATURE OF THE CHARGE (verse 2)

. . . preach the word, be urgent in season and out of season, convince, rebuke, and exhort, be unfailing in patience and in teaching.

Omitting verse 1 for the moment and passing to verse 2, the essence of the charge is in the three words 'Preach the word'. We observe at once that the message Timothy is to communicate is called a 'word', a spoken utterance. Rather it is *the* word, God's word which God has spoken. Paul does not need to specify it further, for Timothy will know at once that it is the body of doctrine which he has heard from Paul and which Paul has now committed to him to pass on to others. It is identical with 'the deposit' of chapter 1. And in this fourth chapter it is equivalent to 'the sound teaching' (3), 'the truth' (4) and 'the faith' (7). It consists of the Old Testament Scriptures, God-breathed and profitable, which Timothy has known from child-hood, together with the teaching of the apostle which Timothy has 'followed', 'learned' and 'firmly believed' (3:10, 14). The same charge is laid upon the church of every age. We have no liberty to invent our message, but only to communicate 'the word' which God has spoken and has now committed to the church as a sacred trust.

Timothy is to 'preach' this word, himself to speak what God has spoken. His responsibility is not just to hear it, and to believe and obey what he hears; nor just to guard it from every falsification; nor just to suffer for it and continue in it; but now to preach it to others. It is good news of salvation for sinners. So he is to proclaim it like a herald in the market-place (*kēryssō*, *cf.* *kēryx* 'a herald' in 1:11). He is to lift up his voice without fear or favour, and boldly to make it known.

Paul goes on to list four marks which are to characterize Timothy's proclamation.

a. An urgent proclamation

The verb *ephistēmi*, 'be urgent', means literally to 'stand by', and so to 'be ready, be on hand' (AG). But here it appears to take on the flavour not just of alertness and eagerness, but of insistence and urgency. 'Never lose your sense of urgency' (JBP). Certainly it is no good preaching in a listless or lackadaisical manner. All true preaching conveys a sense of the urgent importance of what is being preached. The Christian herald knows that he is handling matters of life and death. He is announcing the sinner's plight under the judgment of God, the saving action of God through the death and resurrection of Christ, and the summons to repent and believe. How can he treat such themes with cold indifference? 'Whatever you do,' wrote Richard Baxter, 'let the people see that you are in good earnest . . . You cannot break men's hearts by jesting with them, or telling them a smooth tale, or patching up a gaudy oration. Men will not cast away their dearest pleasures upon a drowsy request of one that seemeth not to mean as he speaks, or to care much whether his request be granted.'[1]

Such urgent preaching, Paul adds, must continue 'in season and out of season'. 'Press it home on all occasions, convenient or inconvenient' (NEB). This injunction is not to be taken as an excuse for the insensitive brashness which has sometimes characterized our evangelism and brought it into disrepute. We have no liberty to barge unceremoniously into other people's privacy or tread clumsily on their corns. No. The occasions Paul has in mind are probably 'welcome or unwelcome' (JB) not for the hearers so much as for the speaker. The translation of the NEB margin emphasizes this: 'be on duty at all times, convenient or inconvenient'. This takes the verb *ephistēmi* in its alternative sense, which is found sometimes in the papyri. It seems, then, that what we are given here is not a biblical warrant for rudeness, but a biblical appeal against laziness.

b. A relevant proclamation

The herald who announces the word is to 'convince, rebuke and exhort'. This suggests three different ways of doing it. For God's word is 'profitable' for a variety of ministries, as Paul has already stated (3:16). It speaks to different men in different situations. The preacher must remember this and be skilful in his use of it.

[1] *The Reformed Pastor*, 1656. (Epworth, 2nd edition revised, 1950), p. 145.

He must 'use argument, reproof, and appeal' (NEB), which is almost a classification of three approaches, intellectual, moral and emotional. For some people are tormented by doubts and need to be convinced by arguments. Others have fallen into sin, and need to be rebuked. Others again are haunted by fears, and need to be encouraged. God's word does all this and more. We are to apply it relevantly.

c. A patient proclamation

Although we are to be *urgent* (longing for people to make a ready response to the word), we are to be 'unfailing in patience' in waiting for it. We must never resort to the use of human pressure techniques, or attempt to contrive a 'decision'. Our responsibility is to be faithful in preaching the word; the results of the proclamation are the responsibility of the Holy Spirit, and we can afford to wait patiently for him to work. We are to be patient in our whole manner as well, for 'the Lord's servant must . . . be . . . kindly to everyone, . . . forbearing, correcting his opponents with gentleness' (2:24, 25). However solemn our commission and urgent our message, there can be no possible justification for a brusque or impatient manner.

d. An intelligent proclamation

We are not only to preach the word but to teach it, or rather to preach it 'with all teaching' (*kēryxon . . . en pasē . . . didachē*). C. H. Dodd has made the whole church familiar with his distinction between *kērygma* and *didachē*, the former being the proclamation of Christ to unbelievers with a summons to repent, and the latter the ethical instruction of converts. The distinction is helpful and important. Yet, as has already been suggested in the comment on 1:11, it can be pressed too rigidly. At least, this verse shows that our *kērygma* must itself contain much *didachē*. Whether our proclamation is intended primarily to convince, rebuke or exhort, it must be a doctrinal ministry.

The Christian pastoral ministry is essentially a teaching ministry, which explains why candidates are required both to be orthodox in their own faith and to have an aptitude for teaching (*e.g.* Tit. 1:9; 1 Tim. 3:2). There is an increasing need, especially as the process of urbanization continues and standards of education rise, for Christian ministers to exercise in the teeming cities of the developing world a systematic expository preaching ministry, to 'proclaim the word . . . with all teaching'. This is precisely what Paul had himself done in Ephesus, as Timothy well knew. For some three years he had continued to teach 'the whole counsel of God' both 'in public and from house to house' (Acts 20:20, 27; *cf.* 19:8–10). Now Timothy must do the same.

Such is Paul's charge to Timothy. He is to preach the word, and as he announces the God-given message to be urgent in his approach, relevant in his application, patient in his manner and intelligent in his presentation.

2. THE BASIS OF THE CHARGE (verses 1, 3–8)

I charge you in the presence of God and of Christ Jesus who is to judge the living and the dead, and by his appearing and his kingdom . . . ³*For the time is coming when people will not endure sound teaching, but having itching ears they will accumulate for themselves teachers to suit their own likings,* ⁴*and will turn away from listening to the truth and wander into myths.* ⁵*As for you, always be steady, endure suffering, do the work of an evangelist, fulfil your ministry.*

⁶*For I am already on the point of being sacrificed; the time of my departure has come.* ⁷*I have fought the good fight, I have finished the race, I have kept the faith.* ⁸*Henceforth there is laid up for me the crown of righteousness, which the Lord, the righteous judge, will award to me on that Day, and not only to me but also to all who have loved his appearing.*

It has already become apparent in early chapters of this letter both that Timothy was diffident by disposition and that the times in which he lived and worked were—to say the least—unpropitious. He must have quailed as he read the apostle's solemn charge to him to keep preaching the word. He would be tempted to shrink from such a responsibility. So Paul does more than issue a charge; he adds incentives. He bids Timothy look in three directions— first at Jesus Christ the coming judge and king, secondly at the contemporary scene, and thirdly at him, Paul, the aged prisoner approaching martyrdom.

a. The coming Christ (verse 1)

Paul is not issuing his charge in his own name or on his own authority but 'in the presence of God and of Christ Jesus' and therefore conscious of the divine direction and approval. Perhaps the strongest of all incentives to faithfulness is the sense of a commission from God. If Timothy can only be assured that he is the servant of the most high God and an ambassador of Jesus Christ, and that Paul's challenge to him is God's challenge, then nothing will deflect him from his task.

The main emphasis of this first verse, however, is not so much on the presence of God as on the coming of Christ. It is evident that Paul still believes in Christ's personal return. He wrote of it in his earliest letters, especially those to the Thessalonian church. Although he now knows that he will die before it takes place, yet still at the end of his ministry he looks forward to it, lives in the light of it and describes Christians as those who love Christ's appearing (8). He is sure that Christ will make a visible 'appearing' (the word is *epiphaneia* in verses 1 and 8), and that when he appears he will both 'judge the living and the dead' and consummate 'his kingdom' or reign.

Now these three truths—the appearance, the judgment and the kingdom—should be as clear and certain an expectation to us as they were to Paul and Timothy. They cannot fail to exert a powerful influence on our ministry. For both those who preach the word and those who listen to it must give an account to Christ when he appears.

b. The contemporary scene (verses 3–5)

Notice the word 'for' or 'because' (*gar*) which introduces this paragraph. Paul is giving a second basis on which to ground his charge. It is another future event, not now the coming of Christ but, before that end point, the coming of dark and difficult days. Although the apostle seems to be anticipating that the situation will deteriorate, it is also plain from this paragraph and from what he has written earlier that such a time has already begun for Timothy. It is in the light of this contemporary scene that he issues further directions.

What are these times like? One characteristic is singled out, namely that people cannot bear the truth. Paul expresses it negatively and positively, and states it twice: They 'will not endure sound teaching, but . . . accumulate . . . teachers to suit their own likings' (3). They 'will turn away from listening to the truth and wander into myths' (4). In other words, they cannot stand the truth and refuse to listen to it. Instead, they find teachers to suit the speculative fancies into which they are determined to wander. It all has to do with their ears, which (in the Greek sentence) are mentioned twice. They suffer from a peculiar pathological condition called 'itching ears', 'an itch for novelty'.[1] AG explain that the expression is a figure of speech for that kind of curiosity which 'looks for interesting and spicy bits of information'. Further, 'this itching is relieved by the messages of the new teachers'. In fact what the people do is stop their ears against the truth (*cf.* Acts 7:57) and open them to any teacher who will relieve their tickle by scratching it.

Notice that what they reject is 'the sound teaching' (3) or 'the truth' (4), and what they prefer is 'their own likings' (3) or 'myths' (4). They thus substitute their fancy for God's revelation. The criterion by which they judge teachers is not (as it should be) God's word but their own subjective taste. Worse still, they do not first listen and then decide whether what they have heard is true; they first decide what they want to hear and then select teachers who will oblige by toeing their line.

How is Timothy to react to this? One might guess that such a desperate situation should silence him. If men cannot bear the truth and will not listen to it, surely the prudent course will be for him to hold his peace? But Paul reaches the opposite conclusion. For the third time he uses those two little monosyllables *su de*, 'but as for you' (5; *cf.* 3:10, 14). He repeats his call to Timothy to be different. He must not take his lead from the prevailing fashions of the day.

Now follow four staccato commands which seem to be deliberately framed in relation to the situation in which Timothy finds himself and to the kind of people to whom he is called to minister.

1. Because the people are unstable in mind and conduct,

[1] Ellicott, p. 160.

Timothy is above everything else always to 'be steady'. Literally, *nēphō* means to be sober, and figuratively to 'be free from every form of mental and spiritual drunkenness' and so to 'be well-balanced, self-controlled' (AG). When men and women get intoxicated with heady heresies and sparkling novelties, ministers must keep 'calm and sane' (NEB).

2. Although the people will not listen to the sound teaching, Timothy must persist in teaching it and so be prepared to 'endure suffering' on account of the truth he refuses to compromise. Whenever the biblical faith becomes unpopular, ministers are sorely tempted to mute those elements which give most offence.

3. Because the people are woefully ignorant of the true evangel, Timothy is to 'do the work of an evangelist'. It is not clear whether the reference is to a specialist ministry such as is implied in the only other New Testament passages where the word occurs (Acts 21:8; Eph. 4:11). The alternative is to interpret it of anybody who preaches the gospel and witnesses to Christ. In either case Paul is bidding Timothy: 'make the preaching of the Good News your life's work' (JB). The good news is not just to be preserved against distortion; it is to be spread abroad.

4. Even if the people forsake Timothy's ministry in favour of teachers who tickle their fancy, Timothy is to 'fulfil' his 'ministry'. The same verb is used when Paul and Barnabas had completed the relief work which they went to Jerusalem to do. 'They had fulfilled their mission', Luke writes (Acts 12:25). Just so Timothy must persevere until his task is accomplished.

Thus Paul's four words of command, although different in detail, convey the same general message. Those difficult days, in which it was hard to gain a hearing for the gospel, were not to discourage Timothy; nor to deter him from his ministry; nor to induce him to trim his message to suit his hearers; still less to silence him altogether; but rather to spur him on to preach the more. It should be the same with us. The harder the times and the deafer the people, the clearer and more persuasive our proclamation must be. As Calvin puts it, 'the more determined men become to despise the teaching of Christ, the more zealous should godly ministers be to assert it and the more strenuous their efforts to preserve it entire, and more than that, by their diligence to ward off Satan's attacks'.[1]

c. *The aged apostle* (verses 6-8)

The third ground of the apostle's charge is yet another coming event, namely his own martyrdom. The link between this paragraph and verse 5 which precedes it is plain. Paul's argument runs like this: 'But as for *you*, Timothy, *you* must fulfil *your* ministry, for *I* am already on the point of death.' It is all the more vital for Timothy to continue and complete his ministry because the apostle's life-work has reached completion and is about to close. As Joshua had followed Moses, and Solomon David, and Elisha Elijah, so now Timothy must follow Paul.

The apostle uses two vivid figures of speech to portray his coming death, one taken from the language of sacrifice and the other (probably) of boats. First, 'I am already on the point of being sacrificed.' Or 'Already my life is being poured out on the altar' (NEB). He likens his life to a libation or drink offering. So imminent does he believe his martyrdom to be that he speaks of the sacrifice as having already begun. He goes on: 'the time of my departure has come'. 'Departure' (*analysis*) seems to have become a regular word for death, but we need not necessarily conclude from this that its metaphorical origin had been entirely forgotten. It means 'loosing' and could be used either of striking a tent (which Lock favours,[2] because of the soldier's 'I have fought a good fight' in the following verse) or of 'release from shackles' (which Simpson mentions),[3] or of untying a boat from its moorings. The last is certainly the most picturesque of the three possibilities. The two images then to some extent correspond,[4] for the end of this life (outpoured as a libation) is the beginning of another (putting out to sea). Already the anchor is weighed, the ropes are slipped, and the boat is about to set sail for another shore. Now, before the great adventure of his new voyage begins, he looks back over his ministry of about 30 years. He

---

[1] Calvin, p. 334.   [2] Lock, p. 111.   [3] Simpson, p. 154.

[4] It is interesting that Paul used both metaphors during an earlier imprisonment, in which he had also faced the possibility of death (Phil. 2:17; 1:23).

describes it—factually not boastfully—in three terse expressions.

First, 'I have fought the good fight'. The words could equally well be translated 'I have run the great race' (NEB), for *agōn* denoted any contest involving exertion, whether a race or a fight. But since the next phrase clearly alludes to the race or course he has finished, it seems probable that Paul is again combining the soldier and athlete metaphors (as in 2:3–5), or at least the wrestling and running metaphors.

Next, he writes, 'I have finished the race'. Some years previously, speaking to the elders of the very Ephesian church over which Timothy was now presiding, Paul had expressed his ambition to do just this. 'I do not account my life of any value,' he had declared, 'nor as precious to myself, if only I may accomplish my course and the ministry which I received from the Lord Jesus . . .' (Acts 20:24). Now he is able to say that he has done so. Both the verb and the noun he uses are the same. 'What had been a purpose was now a retrospect,' comments N. J. D. White.[1] He could use the perfect tense in each of these three expressions, as Jesus had done in the upper room,[2] because the end was so clearly in sight.

Thirdly, 'I have kept the faith'. This may conceivably mean 'I have kept faith with my Master'.[3] But in the context of this letter, which emphasizes so strongly the importance of guarding the deposit of revealed truth, it is more likely that Paul is affirming his faithfulness in this respect. 'I have safely preserved, as a guardian or steward, the gospel treasure committed to my trust.'

So the work of the apostle, and to a lesser extent of every gospel preacher and teacher, is pictured as fighting a fight, running a race, guarding a treasure. Each involves labour, sacrifice and even danger. In all three Paul has been faithful to the end.

Now nothing remains for him but the prize, which he terms 'the crown (or better 'garland') of righteousness', which is 'laid up' for him and which will be given him at the winning post 'on that Day'. Though intrinsically valueless, being made of ever-

---

[1] White, p. 178.
[2] Jn. 17:4: 'having accomplished the work which thou gavest me to do'.
[3] Lock, p. 111.

green leaves rather than of silver or gold, the garlands won by victors in the Greek games were greatly prized. 'Many a little town in those days', writes Bishop Handley Moule, 'took down a piece of its white wall in order that its son, crowned with the crown of the isthmus or of Olympia, might enter it *by a gate unused before*.'[1] The crown which Paul anticipates he calls 'righteousness' (*dikaiosynē*). From his pen the word would most naturally mean 'justification'. But perhaps here it has a slightly different legal connotation, and is in deliberate contrast to the sentence he is expecting any day to receive from a human judge in a human court. The Emperor Nero may declare him guilty and condemn him to death, but there will soon come a 'magnificent reversal of Nero's verdict'[2] when 'the Lord, the righteous judge', declares him righteous.

The same vindication by Christ also awaits 'all who have loved his appearing'. This is not, of course, a doctrine of justification by good works. It is hardly necessary to emphasize Paul's continuing conviction that salvation is a free gift of God's grace, 'not in virtue of our works but in virtue of his own purpose and . . . grace' (1:9). The crown of righteousness is awarded to all those who 'have set their hearts on his coming appearance' (NEB), not because this is a meritorious attitude to adopt but because it is a sure evidence of justification. The unbeliever, being unjustified, dreads the coming of Christ (if he believes in it or thinks about it at all). Being unready for it, he will shrink in shame from Christ at his coming. The believer, on the other hand, having been justified, looks forward to Christ's coming and has set his heart upon it. Being ready for it, he will have boldness when Christ appears (1 Jn. 2:28). Only those who have entered by faith into the benefit of Christ's first coming are eagerly awaiting his second (*cf*. Heb. 9:28).

This then is 'Paul the aged', as he has described himself a year or two previously in his letter to Philemon (verse 9). He has fought the good fight, finished the race and kept the faith. His lifeblood is on the point of being poured out. His little boat is about to set sail. He is eagerly awaiting his crown. These facts are to be Timothy's third spur to faithfulness.

Our God is the God of history. 'God is working his purpose

[1] Moule, p. 145.   [2] Simpson, p. 157.

out, as year succeeds to year.' 'He buries his workmen, but carries
on his work.' The torch of the gospel is handed down by each
generation to the next. As the leaders of the former generation
die, it is all the more urgent for those of the next generation to
step forward bravely to take their place. Timothy's heart must
have been profoundly moved by this exhortation from Paul the
old warrior who had led him to Christ. Who led you to Christ?
Is he growing old? The man who introduced me to Christ is
now living in retirement (though an active one!). We cannot
rest for ever on the leadership of the preceding generation. The
day comes when we must step into their shoes and ourselves
take the lead. That day had come for Timothy. It comes to all
of us in time.

So then, in view of the coming of Christ to judgment, of the
contemporary world's distaste for the gospel and of the imprisoned apostle's imminent death, the latter's charge to Timothy
had a note of solemn urgency: *Preach the word!*

3. AN ILLUSTRATION OF THE CHARGE (verses 9–22)

Do your best to come to me soon. [10] *For Demas, in love with this present
world, has deserted me and gone to Thessalonica; Crescens has gone to
Galatia, Titus to Dalmatia.* [11] *Luke alone is with me. Get Mark and
bring him with you; for he is very useful in serving me.* [12] *Tychicus I have
sent to Ephesus.* [13] *When you come, bring the cloak that I left with
Carpus at Troas, also the books, and above all the parchments.* [14] *Alexander the coppersmith did me great harm; the Lord will requite him for
his deeds.* [15] *Beware of him yourself, for he strongly opposed our message.*
[16] *At my first defence no one took my part; all deserted me. May it
not be charged against them!* [17] *But the Lord stood by me and gave me
strength to proclaim the message fully, that all the Gentiles might hear it.
So I was rescued from the lion's mouth.* [18] *The Lord will rescue me from
every evil and save me for his heavenly kingdom. To him be the glory for
ever and ever. Amen.*

[19] *Greet Prisca and Aquila, and the household of Onesiphorus.*
[20] *Erastus remained at Corinth; Trophimus I left ill at Miletus.* [21] *Do
your best to come before winter. Eubulus sends greetings to you, as do
Pudens and Linus and Claudia and all the brethren.*

[22] *The Lord be with your spirit. Grace be with you.*

Paul does more than issue Timothy, from what might seem the safe distance of his prison cell, with an apostolic charge to preach the word; he gives him an illustration of it from his own example. For he himself has preached the word, not just throughout his ministry but very recently, boldly proclaiming the gospel in court when on trial for his life before imperial Rome.

Before we are ready to consider the details of this remarkable proclamation, however, we must understand the circumstances in which it took place.

From his majestic survey of the past ('I have fought the good fight . . .') and his confident anticipation of the future ('henceforth there is laid up for me the crown . . .') Paul returns in thought to the present and to his personal predicament. For the great apostle Paul was also a creature of flesh and blood, a man of like nature and passions with ourselves. Although he has finished his course and is awaiting his crown, he is still a frail human being with ordinary human needs. He describes his plight in prison, and expresses in particular his loneliness.

Several factors contributed to his sense of isolation, and these he openly describes. He had been deserted by his friends (9–13); he had been opposed by Alexander the coppersmith (14, 15); and he had been unsupported at his first defence (16–18).

a. Deserted by his friends (verses 9–13 and 19–21)

It is quite true that Paul has not been left entirely friendless. This becomes clear if at this point we glance on to the end of the chapter. Paul mentions here, first, his friends overseas (19), and he sends them a message of greeting. Prisca and Aquila, whom he has called his 'fellow workers in Christ Jesus' (Rom. 16:3) and with whom he stayed in Corinth (Acts 18:2; 1 Cor. 16:19), are evidently still in Ephesus where we last heard of them in the Acts record (18:26). So is 'the household of Onesiphorus', although, as was suggested in the comment on 1:16–18, it seems that Onesiphorus himself is still separated from his family and in Rome.

Paul next sends Timothy items of news about two other mutual friends (20). Erastus, he says, 'remained at Corinth'. It may well be right to identify him with the Erastus who is described as Corinth's 'city treasurer' (Rom. 16:23) and with the Erastus whom Paul sent with Timothy into Macedonia (Acts 19:22). The fact that Paul needs to inform Timothy that he had stayed in Corinth suggests that after Paul's re-arrest he may have accompanied the prisoner as far as Corinth on his way to Rome. The other news item concerns Trophimus, who was a native of Ephesus and had been one of Paul's companions during his third missionary journey at least in Greece and Troas and on the voyage to Jerusalem (Acts 20:1–5; 21:29). We do not know the circumstances in which Paul left him ill at Miletus, the port near Ephesus.

In these final verses of the letter the apostle also mentions some Christians in Rome, who send their greetings to Timothy. He gives the names of three men—Eubulus, Pudens and Linus (the latter just possibly the Linus whom Irenaeus and Eusebius mention as the first Bishop of Rome following the martyrdom of Peter and Paul)—and of one lady, Claudia, and then mentions 'all the brethren'. It seems likely, since Paul knows some of their names and can send greetings from them to Timothy, that they have visited him in prison.

Nevertheless, the apostle feels himself terribly cut off and abandoned, exiled from the churches he founded and from the people in them he knows and loves. More poignant still is the fact that a number of his close circle of travelling companions have—for a variety of reasons—left him or become separated from him. It is their fellowship that he misses more than anybody's. In verses 10 and 12 he mentions four in particular, Demas, Crescens, Titus and Tychicus.

The desertion of Demas is obviously extremely painful to Paul. He was previously one of his close associates or 'fellow workers'. In the two other New Testament verses in which he is mentioned his name is coupled with Luke's (Col. 4:14; Phm. 24). But now, instead of setting his love on Christ's future appearing (8), he has fallen 'in love with this present world' (literally, 'age'). The details are not divulged. Bishop Moule may have been right to guess that he was 'smitten with cowardice in that reign of terror'.[1] The other three are not censured for their departure. Crescens, whose name does not appear elsewhere in the New Testament,

[1] Moule, p. 150.

has 'gone to Galatia' (perhaps here meaning Gaul), and Titus, who must by now have finished his task in Crete, has travelled to Dalmatia on the Eastern Adriatic coast. No reason is given for these movements. Of Tychicus, however, Paul says: 'I have sent' him 'to Ephesus' (12). Twice described as 'a beloved brother and faithful minister . . . in the Lord', he has been sent on several responsible missions before, apparently carrying Paul's letters to the Ephesians, to the Colossians and to Titus (Eph. 6:21, 22; Col. 4:7, 8; Tit. 3:12). It looks as if he is now being entrusted with the last of all Paul's letters, this one to Timothy. It may be that Paul also intends him to replace Timothy in Ephesus while the latter is absent visiting Paul in Rome.

Here, then, are four intimate and trusted fellow-labourers whom Paul sorely misses, although (except Demas) their absence is on the Lord's legitimate business. He goes on: 'Luke alone is with me' (11). It is a touching testimony to the unflinching loyalty of the apostle's companion and 'beloved physician' (Col. 4:14). Apart from this solitary exception of Luke, however, for various reasons good and bad Paul is alone in prison. He feels it keenly. He longs and asks for three things: first, for people to keep him company; secondly, for a cloak to keep him warm; thirdly, for books and parchments to keep him occupied.

First, companions. He bids Timothy: 'Get Mark and bring him with you' (11). Mark had been a deserter on the first missionary journey (Acts 12:25; 13:13; 15:38, 39). Later, however, he was restored (Col. 4:10; Phm. 24; 1 Pet. 5:13), and now he could be 'very useful in serving' Paul.

But above all Paul yearns for Timothy himself. 'Do your best to come to me soon', he writes (9). 'Do your best to come before winter' (21). If he is ever to see Timothy again and enjoy his friendship, then Timothy must come soon (while he is still alive) and in any case before winter (when navigation would be impossible). So twice he urges him to do his best to come. We must not play down the urgency of Paul's affectionate desire to see Timothy. The same apostle who has set his love and hope upon the coming of Christ (8), nevertheless also longs for the coming of Timothy. 'I long night and day to see you,' he has written at the beginning of his letter, 'that I may be filled with joy' (1:4). The two longings are not incompatible. One sometimes meets super-spiritual people who claim that they never feel lonely and have no need of human friends, for the companionship of Christ satisfies all their needs. But human friendship is the loving provision of God for mankind. It was God himself who said in the beginning: 'it is not good that the man should be alone' (Gn. 2:18). Wonderful as are both the presence of the Lord Jesus every day and the prospect of his coming on the last day, they are not intended to be a substitute for human friendships.

Warm clothing is necessary to Paul, as well as companionship. So he urges Timothy: 'When you come, bring the cloak that I left with Carpus at Troas' (13). It seems probable that the *phailonēs* ('cloak') was the equivalent of the Latin *paenula*, 'an outer garment of heavy material, circular in shape with a hole in the middle for the head.'[1] It was no doubt in anticipation of the coming winter (21) that Paul felt the need of the extra warmth it could give him. But who Carpus was and why Paul left his belongings with him in Troas, we can only guess. Bishop Moule conjectures that it was in the house of Carpus at Troas both that the 'memorable Eucharist' was held (Acts 20:1 ff.) and that years later Paul was arrested and carried off, with no opportunity to gather his possessions together.[2]

The third necessity Paul mentions is 'the books, and above all the parchments' (verse 13). The difference between the two is probably that the former were made of papyrus rather than parchment. These papyrus rolls may have been writing materials or his correspondence or some official documents, even perhaps his certificate of Roman citizenship. The parchments may conceivably have been unused (NEB, 'my notebooks'). But it seems more probable that they were 'books' of some kind, and the most likely guess is 'Paul's version of the Old Testament in Greek, no small burden to carry around',[3] and/or 'possibly official copies of the Lord's words or early narratives of his life'.[4]

These, then, were Paul's three conscious needs. Later he says that during his first defence in court 'the Lord stood by me and gave me strength' (17), and no doubt he enjoyed the companion-

[1] Guthrie, p. 173. [2] Moule, pp. 157 f.
[3] Hanson, p. 102. [4] Lock, p. 118.

ship and strength of the Lord Jesus in his dungeon as well. Yet the help he obtained from his Lord was indirect as well as direct. He did not despise the use of means. Nor should we. When our spirit is lonely, we need friends. When our body is cold, we need clothing. When our mind is bored, we need books. To admit this is not unspiritual; it is human. These are the natural needs of mortal men and women. As Bishop Moule wisely says, man is 'never for one moment denaturalized by grace'.[1] We must not, then, deny our humanity or frailty, or pretend that we are made of other stuff than dust.

Of course some Christians today scorn reading and study altogether, and assert that they would not feel the need of books at any time, let alone in prison. Let Calvin answer them: 'Still more does this passage refute the madness of the fanatics who despise books and condemn all reading and boast only of their *enthusiasmous*, their private inspirations by God. But we should note that this passage commends continual reading to all godly men as a thing from which they can profit.'[2]

Several commentators point out the historical parallel between Paul's imprisonment in Rome and William Tyndale's in Belgium nearly fifteen centuries later. Here is Handley Moule's description of Tyndale and quotation from his letter:

'In 1535, immured by the persecutor at Vilvorde in Belgium, he wrote, not long before his fiery martyrdom, a Latin letter to the Marquis of Bergen, Governor of the Castle: "I entreat your lordship, and that by the Lord Jesus, that if I must remain here for the winter you would beg the Commissary to be so kind as to send me, from the things of mine which he has, a warmer cap; I feel the cold painfully in my head. Also a warmer cloak, for the cloak I have is very thin. He has a woollen shirt of mine, if he will send it. But most of all, my Hebrew Bible, Grammar and Vocabulary, that I may spend my time in that pursuit." '[3]

b. Opposed by Alexander the coppersmith (verses 14, 15)

The second contributing factor to Paul's ordeal was the fierce opposition he had sustained to himself and his message from a

[1] Moule, p. 152.   [2] Calvin, p. 341.   [3] Moule, pp. 158 f.

man named *Alexander*. We know that his trade was that of a 'coppersmith', or worker in bronze, for Paul so describes him. But we do not know his identity. It is improbable that Alexander the coppersmith was the same person as Alexander the heretic (1 Tim. 1:20) or Alexander the orator (Acts 19:33), for the name was a common one. Nor do we know what the 'great harm' was which he had done to the apostle. A. T. Hanson points out that, literally translated, Alexander 'informed many evil things against me' and that 'the regular word for an informer is connected with this verb'.[1] So some commentators suggest that Alexander was the informer responsible for Paul's second arrest. If this happened at Troas, it might explain why Timothy, who will pass through Troas on his journey to Rome (13), is warned: 'beware of him yourself'. But Alexander did more than inform: 'he strongly opposed our message'. We may be quite sure that it was Paul's concern for the truth of the message, and not personal pique or vindictiveness, which led him to express his belief (it is a statement according to the best MSS, not a wish or a prayer): 'the Lord will requite him for his deeds.'

c. Unsupported at his first defence (verses 16–18)

Some have thought that Paul's 'first defence' is a reference to his first imprisonment and that the proclamation of the word to the Gentiles (which he mentions in the following verse) was due to his release from this imprisonment.[2] The context seems, however, to require a reference to some more recent event. So most commentators understand his *first defence* to have been the first hearing or *prima actio* of his case, 'the preliminary investigation preceding the formal trial'.[3]

Now Roman law would have permitted him to employ an advocate and call witnesses. But, as Alfred Plummer puts it, 'among all the Christians in Rome there was not one who would stand at his side in court either to speak on his behalf, or to advise him in the conduct of his case, or to support him by a demonstration of sympathy'.[4] 'At my first defence no one took my part; all deserted me.' Yet if ever an accused man needed help it was now.

---

[1] Hanson, p. 102. [2] So Eusebius II.22.1–8.
[3] Guthrie, p. 175. [4] Plummer, p. 420.

We are not told what charges had been laid against him. But
we know from Tacitus, Pliny and other contemporary writers
the kind of allegations which were being made against Christians
at that time. They were supposed to be guilty of horrid crimes
against the state and against civilized society. They were accused
of 'atheism' (because they eschewed idolatry and emperor-
worship), of cannibalism (because they spoke of eating Christ's
body), and even of a general 'hatred of the human race' (because
of their supposed disloyalty to Caesar and perhaps because they
had renounced the popular pleasures of sin). It may be that some
of these charges were being levelled against Paul. Whatever the
case for the prosecution, he had no-one to defend him but himself. Either because Christian friends could not or would not, he
was unsupported and alone.

This moment, one might cautiously say, was Paul's Geth-
semane. Of course his agony was different from Christ's. Yet like
his Master before him he had to face his ordeal alone, for at the
time of his greatest need he could say 'all deserted me', as it is
written of Christ 'they all forsook him and fled' (Mk. 14:50).
Lock goes even further and, noting nine verbal similarities
between Psalm 22 and verses 10 and 16–18 of this chapter, asks:
'had St. Paul, like his Master, been saying this Psalm in the hour
of his desertion?'[1] Certainly, again like his Master, he prayed
that their sin might 'not be charged against them'. There is no
need, incidentally, to make out that there is an irreconcilable
discrepancy between this prayer and the statement about
Alexander two verses previously. The cases were quite different.
For Alexander had actually spoken against the gospel from
deliberate malice, whereas Paul's friends in Rome had failed to
speak at all, and their silence was due not to malice but to fear.

Nevertheless, once more like his Master, Paul knew that he
was *not* alone. In anticipation of the coming desertion, Jesus said,
'the hour is coming, indeed it has come, when you will be
scattered, every man to his home, and will leave me alone; yet I
am not alone, for the Father is with me' (Jn. 16:32). Similarly
Paul could say that, although 'all deserted me' (16), yet 'the Lord
stood by me and gave me strength' (17). Christ's presence at
Paul's side and his gift to him of inward strength (the verb is

[1] Lock, p. 116.

endynamoō as in 2:1 and Phil. 4:13) both fortified him to preach the gospel to all the Gentiles present and led to his rescue (at least temporarily) 'from the lion's mouth'.

There is much speculation about the identity of the 'lion'. We can be certain that there is no reference to the lions of the amphitheatre, for as a Roman citizen there was never any question that this might be his fate. The early Greek commentators believed that Paul was referring obliquely to Nero, 'on account of his cruel nature',[1] and A. T. Hanson points out that, according to Josephus, the news of the Emperor Tiberius' death in AD 37 'reached Herod Agrippa in the cryptic form "the lion is dead" '.[2] Other guesses are that the lion is Satan (as in 1 Pet. 5:8), or Paul's human prosecutor in court, or death, or, more generally still, the great danger in which his enemies had placed him (as in Pss. 22:21; 35:17). At all events Paul emerges from this incident as a New Testament Daniel for whose protection the Lord shut the lion's mouth. In the future too, Paul goes on confidently, 'the Lord will rescue me', not indeed from death (for he is expecting to die, 6), but 'from every evil' outside God's permitted will. He will also 'save me for his heavenly kingdom', though Nero may soon dispatch me from my earthly kingdom.

We are now in a position to see what a superb illustration the apostle is giving Timothy of his charge to 'preach the word'. Paul is on trial for his life. He has been deserted by his friends (who have left him in the lurch or been unable to help him), opposed by his enemies and unsupported in his trial by any barrister or witness. So he is alone. Surely now he will think of himself for a change? Surely now he will betray at least a little self-pity? Surely now he will defend himself and plead his cause? Perhaps he did answer the charges laid against him, for he refers to the trial as his 'defence' (16). Yet even now, although in grave personal danger, facing the probability of a death sentence, his overmastering concern is not himself but Christ, not to be a witness in his own defence but a witness to Christ, not to plead his own cause but the cause of Jesus Christ.

In one of the highest tribunals of the empire, before his judges and perhaps before the emperor himself, no doubt with a large crowd of the general public present, Paul 'preached the word'.

[1] Eusebius, II.22.4.   [2] Hanson, p. 103.

Or, as he himself expresses it: 'the Lord stood by me and gave me strength to proclaim the message fully, that all the Gentiles might hear it'. If ever there has been a sermon preached 'out of season', this was it!

All he tells us about its content is that he 'fully preached the *kērygma*'. That is, he took the opportunity to expound the gospel in its fullness, the good news of Jesus Christ incarnate, crucified, risen, reigning and coming again. Only because of this could he claim as he has done 'I have finished the race' (7).

Alfred Plummer gives a graphic description of the scene as he envisages it:

'It is quite possible that this event, which the Apostle of the Gentiles regards as the completing act of his own mission and ministry, took place in the forum itself . . . But at any rate it would be held in a court to which the public had access; and the Roman public at this time was the most representative in the world . . . In that representative city and before that representative audience he preached Christ; and through those who were present and heard him the fact would be made known throughout the civilized world that in the imperial city and before the imperial bench the Apostle of Christ had proclaimed the coming of his kingdom.'[1]

This, then, is to be Timothy's model. He has in past days followed Paul in his doctrine, conduct and sufferings (3:10, 11); he could safely follow Paul's example in this also. For in issuing the solemn charge to Timothy to preach the word, and do it urgently, Paul has not evaded the challenge himself. On the contrary, he has enforced his charge, not only from Christ's coming, the contemporary scene and his impending death, but also by the shining example he has himself just set in the imperial court at a moment of great personal loneliness and peril.

d. Conclusion

Underlying this whole letter is Paul's basic conviction that God has spoken through his prophets and apostles, and that this

[1] Plummer pp. 425 f.

unique revelation—'the faith', 'the truth', 'the word', 'the gospel', 'the sound teaching'—has been committed to the church as a sacred treasure or 'deposit'.

Now the apostle, who throughout his three decades of active ministry has faithfully delivered to others what he himself had received, is on his death bed. He is on the very point of being sacrificed. He seems to have caught a glimpse with his mind's eye of the gleaming steel of the executioner's sword. So he burns with a passionate longing that Timothy, his young but trusted lieutenant, will step into his shoes, carry on from where he has had to stop, and pass on the torch to others.

Paul is fully alert to the difficulties, however, both internal and external. Timothy himself is inexperienced, infirm and shy. The world's opposition is strong and subtle. And behind these things stands the devil, bent on 'taking men alive' and keeping them prisoner. For the devil hates the gospel and uses all his strength and cunning to obstruct its progress, now by perverting it in the mouths of those who preach it, now by frightening them into silence through persecution or ridicule, now by persuading them to advance beyond it into some fancy novelty, now by making them so busy with defending the gospel that they have no time to proclaim it.

So then, knowing the sacred deposit entrusted to him, the imminence of his own martyrdom, the natural weaknesses of Timothy, the opposition of the world and the extreme subtlety of Satan, Paul issues to Timothy his fourfold charge regarding the gospel—to guard it (because it is a priceless treasure), to suffer for it (because it is a stumbling-block to the proud), to continue in it (because it is the truth of God) and to proclaim it (because it is good news of salvation).

Timothy was called to be faithful in his generation; where are the men and women who will be faithful in ours? They are urgently needed. No doubt our response will be: 'who is sufficient for these things?' If so, we need to consider two brief expressions in the final verses of the letter, which I have so far passed by.

First in verse 22: 'The Lord be with your spirit. Grace be with you.' These are the very last recorded words of the apostle. If he has been dictating thus far (perhaps to Luke), possibly now he takes the pen himself and writes this as his autograph. May 'the Lord be with you' (singular), he prays, as he has been with me during my trial (17). And may 'grace (the word in which all Paul's theology is distilled) be with you'. This time the pronoun 'you' is plural, which 'recognizes that the letter was in fact destined for public use'.[1] It was directed to the whole church. It is directed to us today.

Then in verse 18 we read, 'To him be the glory for ever and ever. Amen.' It would be difficult to find a better summary than these two sentences of the apostle's life and ambition. First, he received grace from Christ. Then he returned glory to Christ. 'From him grace; to him glory.' In all our Christian life and service we should desire no other philosophy than this.

[1] Barrett, p. 125.

The Bible Speaks Today

Series Editors: J. A. Motyer (OT)
John R. W. Stott (NT)

The Message of 2 Timothy
Guard the Gospel

Titles in this series